Cambridge Elements ≡

Elements in England in the Early Medieval World
edited by
Megan Cavell
University of Birmingham
Rory Naismith
University of Cambridge
Winfried Rudolf
University of Göttingen
Emily V. Thornbury
Yale University

T0334369

VISIONS OF HIERARCHY AND INEQUALITY IN EARLY MEDIEVAL ENGLAND

Stuart Pracy
University of Exeter

CAMBRIDGE
UNIVERSITY PRESS

Shaftesbury Road, Cambridge CB2 8EA, United Kingdom

One Liberty Plaza, 20th Floor, New York, NY 10006, USA

477 Williamstown Road, Port Melbourne, VIC 3207, Australia

314–321, 3rd Floor, Plot 3, Splendor Forum, Jasola District Centre, New Delhi – 110025, India

103 Penang Road, #05–06/07, Visioncrest Commercial, Singapore 238467

Cambridge University Press is part of Cambridge University Press & Assessment, a department of the University of Cambridge.

We share the University's mission to contribute to society through the pursuit of education, learning and research at the highest international levels of excellence.

www.cambridge.org
Information on this title: www.cambridge.org/9781009494571

DOI: 10.1017/9781009308342

First published 2024

A catalogue record for this publication is available from the British Library

ISBN 978-1-009-49457-1 Hardback
ISBN 978-1-009-30836-6 Paperback
ISSN 2632-203X (online)
ISSN 2632-2021 (print)

Visions of Hierarchy and Inequality in Early Medieval England

Elements in England in the Early Medieval World

DOI: 10.1017/9781009308342
First published online: November 2024

Stuart Pracy
University of Exeter

Author for correspondence: Stuart Pracy, s.pracy@exeter.ac.uk

Abstract: This Element examines the sociopolitical hierarchy of England in the tenth and eleventh centuries, focusing upon the plasticity of the boundary between the ranks of ceorl and thegn. Offering a nuanced analysis of terms such as *ceorl* and *thegn* in both early medieval texts and modern scholarship, the Element highlights the mechanisms that allowed these non-institutional signifiers to hold such social weight while conferring few tangible benefits. To better describe relative social positions, the author argues that a compound method is preferable, supporting this proposal via a thorough deconstruction of writings by Archbishop Wulfstan II of York – responsible for many of scholars' ideas about rank in the period – and the examination of sources that evidence a blurring of 'middling' social boundaries across the two centuries under discussion. Together, these strands of interrogation allow for a fuller understanding of how status was constructed in early medieval England.

Keywords: early medieval England, thegn, ceorl, status, social history

ISBNs: 9781009494571 (HB), 9781009308366 (PB), 9781009308342 (OC)
ISSNs: 2632-203X (online), 2632-2021 (print)

Contents

1 Introduction

From eleventh-century Ely, Cambridgeshire, survive six short and unique memoranda. It is only by good fortune, and the detective work of several historians across seventy or so years, that these fragments of managerial ephemera have been reunited as BL Add 61735.[1] Collected, they yield a compelling window into the minutiae of local agrarian economies in early medieval England. As Rory Naismith has shown, the hands of four scribes record these entries in a scrappy and rushed English vernacular minuscule, the yellow parchment marked by a brown ink which varies wildly in size and sometimes seems to fall over itself in a rush to make it onto the page.[2] These textual witnesses to the everyday management of monasterial business object-ivise the various transactions and renders which flowed in and out of Ely's institutional grasp.

Among the lists of supplies, such as bean seed, harrows, oxen, and swine, we find evidence of people being redeployed across estates and traded between monasteries. Among others, a woman, madder-keeper, swineherd, and dairy maid were transferred between parties. In a rather unusual fashion, we also find mention that the service of 'cynsiges swystor myleneres' (the sister of Cynsige the Miller) and 'hyringmannum' (hired men) was purchased. All these individ-uals were of low status in the grand scheme of pre-Conquest English society. Yet the plurality of terms is indicative of a scribal tendency towards precision, or, occasionally, imprecision, shaped by an awareness of the complexities of the world around them.

Given that many of the people in question shared a similar state of servitude, one might expect that the scribe would have simply labelled these purchased and traded people as *þeow*, or slaves. This label, however, is not deployed in these fragments. The imprecise terms *man* and *woman* are wielded to solely denote the gender of the people to be transferred. Their rank, beyond their implied unfreedom, is left unspoken. Rather, the scribe chooses to emphasise the roles performed by the madder-keeper, swineherd, and dairy maid on the early medieval estate; functionality defines them. As discussed already, the unnamed sister of Cynsige is differentiated by the occupation of her brother, a miller, while the hired men – who were sometimes employed to temporarily fulfil the services rendered by slaves – were characterised by the payments they received and the fleeting nature of their tenure. Contemporary artefacts bear

---

[1] Naismith, 'The Ely Memoranda', 333–336. The memoranda are written on both sides of a single folio. It survived as three separate scraps which were reunited only in 1979.

[2] Naismith, 'The Ely Memoranda', 342–345.

witness to the intricacy of the early medieval Cambridgeshire fens, which were far from being a society of broad, homogenised categories.

This is, of course, not to say that it was a society in which people did not make use of broad, homogenising categories. To clarify, people simplify matters to expedite the transfer of concepts and improve communication, rounding off the corners of complex identities so that they may be more easily conveyed. The matrix of social interactions was, in fact, very (perhaps infinitely) complicated, and the inhabitants of early medieval England (especially ecclesiasts) distilled these into words which represented these relations. Thus we are presented with the three notorious categories of *laboratores, oratores, and bellatores*: terms which streamlined the messiness of early medieval society and caught an aspect of its essence in a manner that could be deployed within a specific context. This ternary model, a conceit first used in Carolingian France, depicts (male-centric) society as comprised of three pillars: those who work the land, those who pray for the spiritual well-being of all Christians, and those who fight the earthly battles that plague humankind.[3]

Used by the anonymous composer of the Alfredian Old English translation of Boethius's *Consolation of Philosophy* (880 × 950), Ælfric of Eynsham (c.955–c.1010), and Wulfstan II of York (d. 1023), this ternary model retained utility among ecclesiastical commentators in early medieval England.[4] Such sources may, as Paul Hyams puts it, 'tell us most about the fears and hopes of a few elite clerics worrying about the future of salvation' rather than the reality of day-to-day experiences.[5] There was a desire to wrest order from the chaos, and most would agree with Giles Constable that 'the medieval schemas bear little relation to the realities of how people live and interact . . . but . . . reflect a profound need to understand and impose order upon their society'.[6] Still, we know that this concept of the Three Orders made it beyond the cloister. Ælfric of Eynsham discussed this ternary model with a local thegn, so one may assume that it had some cachet among some of the lower nobility.[7] Moreover, the wielding of this concept as a rhetorical device in response to the invasions which beset King Æthelred's regime would seem to suggest some wider social reach.[8] Thus, while the Three Orders model was not necessarily thought by the inhabitants of early medieval England to accurately represent the social complexity of their society,

---

[3] On the Three Orders more generally, see Duby, *The Three Orders*, 42–43; Gurevich, 'Medieval Culture and Mentality'; Oexle, 'Le travail au XIe siècle'. Aron Gurevich and Otto Gerhard Oexle note that it is problematic to draw a boundary between the 'real' and the 'ideological'.

[4] Freedman, *Images*, 22; Powell, 'The "Three-Orders"'.   [5] Hyams, 'Servitude', 130.

[6] Constable, *Three Studies*, 294–295.

[7] Compare Powell, 'The "Three-Orders"'. Timothy Powell contends that the model never reached much beyond the cloistered discourse of the clerical elite.

[8] See Moilanen, 'The Concept of the Three Orders', 1340–1341.

it held weight within the ecclesiastical and lay communities as a vision of an ideal.

This vision of English hierarchical structures depicted for some groups the importance of social boundaries, why they should be upheld, and how this related to individuals' social function. It captured a perceived facet of reality, magnifying a mechanism of social division and expressing a straightforward concept in a way that resonated with what Conrad Leyser calls the '"ought" world' – how certain dominant historical agents thought the world should operate – of noble and ecclesiastical elites.[9] Comparison of the Ely memoranda and the Three Orders model reveals a notable gap between the everyday experience of hierarchy and how it could be conceptualised to elevate an ideal. Accordingly, it might be tempting to leave such social models to one side and focus instead on the day-to-day 'reality'. Leyser, speaking of such issues when approaching late antique and early medieval law, argues that it would be a misstep to dismiss the ought world – most often seen in legal norms – as 'fantasy'. To take the construction of law as an example, he notes that it was the product of 'a register of need, opportunity, and social negotiation'.[10] There was a point of contact between the formal and the informal, the abstract and experience. Legal practice was constantly being reshaped and repurposed to respond to changing interests and demands. Thus, Leyser claimed that a new legal history, which is more expansive than the old, is required.[11] Likewise, an 'expansive' approach to studying hierarchy in early medieval England is also needed. When faced with mounting evidence that points to the complexity of society in the period and the inconsistency of social boundaries, how do we reconcile the 'ideal' and the 'real'?[12] Or, indeed, how do we reconcile our varied scholarly models which stress different aspects of vertical relations and inadvertently reinforce a social taxonomy that was, arguably, only manifest in certain environments?

In response to such difficulties, this Element suggests that the key to navigating the issues which surround any discussion of hierarchy in pre-Conquest England is to embrace the plasticity of social boundaries and utilise taxonomies that suit scholars' various purposes. Binaries may prove useful, but only when approaching social groups along one vector, and even here such approaches often have their limits. In seeking to deconstruct the binary between freedom and unfreedom, Alice Rio has compellingly argued that the binary relationality of these descriptors has misled historians, and that 'grey-area' legal statuses

---

[9] Leyser, 'Introduction', 7. See also Dresch, 'Legalism, Anthropology, and History'.
[10] Leyser, 'Introduction', 7.   [11] Leyser, 'Introduction', 7–8.
[12] For evidence of the plasticity of social boundaries, see Sections 2 and 4.

were not only present but also occasionally desired.[13] Moreover, even those who were free 'ran the risk of being stigmatized as unfree, when in conflict with their lord'.[14] This Element draws out the range of complexities that emerge when one scrutinises the evidence of the social hierarchy in early medieval England, especially focusing on the late ninth, tenth, and eleventh centuries.

Numerous scholars have observed that the division between thegn and ceorl – arguably the second most profound social distinction in early medieval England after that which lay between free and unfree – was sometimes plastic and thus thriving individuals could surmount the gap.[15] One of the first scholars to address the division between thegn and ceorl in detail was the eminent historian Frank Stenton. Beginning with Archbishop Wulfstan II of York's early eleventh-century description of how a ceorl might become a thegn, Stenton sought moments in which this 'thriving' could be found. Though struggling to find any concrete examples of such social movement, Stenton suggested that it likely happened. Still, he lamented that:

> Social history is handicapped by the necessity of working in categories – king's companions, thegns, ceorls. After trying to piece together the fragments of information which illustrate, and sometimes conceal, the position of men described as ceorls in successive phases of Old English history, one is continually reminded that social classes, by their very nature, are really indefinable.[16]

As expected of Stenton, this is a rather perceptive comment. Still, Stenton stuck to a rigid peasant–thegn binary, as seen in his description of the *geneat* – a locally important non-noble who performed some military services – as 'a peasant with some of the characteristics of a mounted retainer'.[17]

James Campbell was the next to probe this boundary, eloquently arguing in 1982 that the gap between nobles and non-nobles was much smaller in early medieval society than is often assumed.[18] Ten years later, Campbell – ever focused on the processes of the early English state – honed in on certain agents and agencies of the state. Focusing on tax, those who took it (i.e. reeves), and the administration of the kingdom, Campbell identified the need for successful systems of administrators and communication. This, he suggests, provided a route for *geneats*, radknights, or riding-men to work their way up to the

---

[13] Rio, '"Half-Free" Categories', 130.   [14] Hyams, 'Servitude', 152.

[15] Stenton, 'The Thriving of the Anglo-Saxon Ceorl'; Campbell, 'Some Agents and Agencies of the Late Anglo-Saxon State'; Faith, *The English Peasantry*, 61–63; Senecal, 'Keeping Up with the Godwinesons'; Fleming, 'The New Wealth'; Williams, *The World before Domesday*, 2–4; Blair, *Building*, 377–378.

[16] Stenton, 'The Thriving of the Anglo-Saxon Ceorl', 392.

[17] Stenton, *First Century*, 125, 129–130.

[18] Campbell, John, and Wormald, *The Anglo-Saxons*, 244.

rank of thegn.[19] In short, he concludes that the acquisition of 'office brought the opportunity for enrichment; in a country so wealthy as eleventh-century England there must have been many such opportunities'.[20] Thus, while Campbell accepts that social movement could occur, he remains wedded to a rather rigid vision of the social hierarchy. That Campbell, an admirer of the 'late Anglo-Saxon state' and advocate of a maximalist interpretation of the region's institutions, should treat social divisions in this manner should be of no surprise.

In 1995, John Gillingham, discussing the existence of a possible proto-gentry in eleventh-century England, observed that 'below the great lords, the earls and king's thegns, there were many layers of society – lesser thegns and thriving freemen, cnihts and geneats – who shared common interests and pursuits'.[21] These were, to all intents and purposes, layers of society which lived as 'gentlemen' and not, as Gillingham was at pains to note, as peasants.[22] Moreover, he suggested that the eleventh century saw changes in thegnly comportment and military culture. While reframing the local landscape of elite status as one of complex and close relationships, he still envisaged it as a place of clearly demarcated, serried ranks.

After this trail of scholarly crumbs, the 2001 volume of *Anglo-Norman Studies* served a nourishing brace of studies on this subject. Articles by Robin Fleming and Christine Senecal examined changing modes in which thegns displayed their status in the tenth and eleventh centuries. Fleming, developing a counterpart to Gillingham's article, desired to come to 'grips with the materiality of genteel life rather than its *mentalité*'.[23] The focus is, therefore, on consumption and the manners by which thegnly elites performed their status. Though Fleming accepts certain individuals, especially townspeople, had the potential to mimic these displays of consumption and live more 'dignified lives', a thegnage was created 'whose purchased lives were nothing like those of the men and women whose backbreaking labour brought them hoards of silver pennies'.[24] While I do not entirely agree that the gap between thegn and labourer was always as insurmountable as one might be tempted to think, Fleming's incisive study neatly draws out the importance of social performance and how it manifested in the period. Senecal, in particular, made several astute observations that (a) 'No single characteristic, or set of characteristics, prescribed who did or did not have aristocratic status in late Anglo-Saxon England'; (b) 'the distinctions between a wealthy peasant and a low-level

---

[19] Campbell, 'Some Agents and Agencies of the Late Anglo-Saxon State', 216–222.

[20] Campbell, 'Some Agents and Agencies of the Late Anglo-Saxon State', 222.

[21] Gillingham, 'Thegns and Knights', 144.   [22] Gillingham, 'Thegns and Knights', 131, 142.

[23] Fleming, 'The New Wealth', 3.   [24] Fleming, 'The New Wealth', 3.

thegn, or even gradations of power among aristocrats themselves, were very blurred'; and (c) that 'aristocrats and would-be aristocrats participated as aggressively as they could in what I will call "thegnly culture", a composite of many habits and activities that were intended to signify social standing'.[25] In one short article of only sixteen pages, Senecal elegantly drew out the amorphous nature of status construction in early medieval England. Despite its insightful nature, the impact of this paper has been relatively minimal, and Senecal herself never revisited the topic.

Eight years later, Ann Williams picked up the baton in her examination of the 'English aristocracy'. With a keen knowledge of the extant sources, Williams illustrates the difficulties of identifying effective boundaries between the various strata of society in her opening discussion of 'Definitions'.[26] While echoing much of Senecal's previous findings, Williams finds fault with Senecal's decision to stress a thegnly concentration on local connections and her minimisation of royal connections.[27] Still, Williams supported the general thrust of Senecal's argument that social divisions were often unclear.[28] A decade passed with minimal discussion of these issues until John Blair's *Building Anglo-Saxon England*. As with Williams's volume, the plasticity of early medieval hierarchy is not the focus of the monograph, but it does receive an extended treatment in his discussion of emergent lords in the tenth century. Given the nature of his research, Blair maps the expression of aristocratic status onto the archaeological evidence.[29] These studies, while extending the body of data from the period that points to the plasticity of the social division between ceorl and thegn, do not help to narrow down how these terms should be applied. Both volumes instead make liberal use of the term *aristocrat*, presumably to avoid the terminological difficulties which arise from *thegn*.[30] However, it is never clarified how the intersection between *aristocrat* and *thegn* should be conceptualised.

Concerning the difficulties of defining the rich and powerful in the early Middle Ages across north-western Europe, François Bougard, Geneviève Bührer-Thierry, and Régine Le Jan argued in 2013 that the concept of elites is the best way to proceed. Acknowledging that the concept of elites may appear 'vague and sometimes irritating', they asserted that 'it is still highly operative for the societies of the early Middle Ages'.[31] The focus should be on defining 'identities and strategies of distinction, which represent just as many different

---

[25] Senecal, 'Keeping Up with the Godwinesons', 251–252.

[26] Williams, *The World before Domesday*, 1–10.

[27] Williams, *The World before Domesday*, 8–10.

[28] Williams, *The World before Domesday*, 7.   [29] Blair, *Building*, 354–380, esp. 377.

[30] On the term *aristocrat*, see Section 2.

[31] Bougard, Bührer-Thierry, and Le Jan, 'Elites in the Early Middle Ages', 767.

factors of recognition and legitimization'.[32] There is much merit to this suggestion, especially as it invites scholars to focus on context and relationality. Indeed, the essay provides numerous observations that are pertinent to this Element more generally, especially in terms of the mechanisms of status-construction. Still, the rather woolly concept of elites does not really get us any further towards establishing a common understanding of the 'upper' ranks of early medieval English society. The concept of elites is perhaps our best option when approaching north-west Europe as a whole, but it leaves much to be desired when examining England alone.

A quarter of a century after Senecal's paper, this Element seeks to fill the lacuna that remains. Building upon her assertion that there was a significant grey area between the binary division of noble and non-noble, thegn and ceorl, it offers a more precise explanation of how individuals were identified as thegns in a shifting social landscape and, importantly, what that meant to social actors. One aspect that Senecal's article overlooked was the problem of wergild, a rather neat system of compensation that linked rank and legal worth – and one that remains something of a sticking point. Drawing out how this aspect of social division was also not firmly aligned with thegnly rank as portrayed in the surviving sources, I posit an alternative way of defining what the rank of thegn actually denoted: it was a non-institutional sociopolitical marker of prestige or, to make it less of a mouthful, a non-institutional honorific.[33] It had no consistent, specific legal weight or required provision of services. The rank of thegn, therefore, potentially signified a great many things about a single person: they partook in a shared mode of demonstrative behaviour linked to nobleness, they provided a form or forms of service, occupied a certain place within society and fulfilled a specific functionality, and they were potentially due a specific level of legal compensation. Nonetheless, few of these things were securely the preserve of thegns. The term *thegn*, I suggest, connoted much but denoted surprisingly little. That the term was potentially used in a liberal and imprecise manner should not raise alarm. In no way should it be thought that the rank of thegn held little social weight nor that it is some mirage of the sources. The sheer prevalence of the term *thegn* in the sources indicates that it retained widespread social traction, conjuring a whole swathe of associations and normative reference points. When used to describe an individual, it implied a lot about their position in society, their behaviours, and their assets. Much of this may generally have turned out to be true. Still, few of these characteristics were *exclusively* indicated by the rank of thegn.

---

[32] Bougard, Bührer-Thierry, and Le Jan, 'Elites in the Early Middle Ages', 767.

[33] I must thank Emily Harless for her helpful feedback which brought about this definition.

Using both textual evidence from the period and drawing on sociological and anthropological models, Section 2 illustrates that social status, and an associated rank, was indicated through a variety of criteria, including items and actions which served to signify social standing to witnesses. Thus, these representational components were key for onlookers when seeking to ascribe a status to an individual. For the rank of thegn, the section surveys the evidence and develops a list of components that helped observers to identify thegns in the period. This list served and serves as a sort of litmus test. The range of positive indicators helped signpost a person's prestige, and there could be a large range of results, from a local thegn all the way to an ealdorman. Yet there was a loose threshold over which someone could be considered a thegn. Thus, as a term, it recognised someone's social calibre but in only an imprecise manner.

Armed with a more nuanced definition, accompanied with an acceptance of the vagaries of status-construction, how can we move forward and ensure that scholars mean the same thing when using the word *thegn*? This is a key issue that permeates the scholarship. The term *thegn* is used to describe a whole swathe of individuals who had remarkably different experiences, yet still enjoyed the same non-institutional honorific. To combat the risk of miscommunication, I argue that a compound method is a preferable solution – that is, we use multiple descriptors to locate individuals along several relevant vectors. For example, we might talk of a lordly ceorl or a dependant thegn. We would be well served by utilising divisions such as lord and peasant, thegn and ceorl, or lord and dependant depending on what we are trying to convey in our academic studies.

Section 3 drives home the point that even contemporaneous, early medieval commentators made use of different models to describe the social landscape which surrounded them depending upon the purpose of their work. This is a rather fundamental observation that any undergraduate should know: the purpose that lay behind an author's work shaped the lens through which they viewed their subject. Nonetheless, the ramifications of this simple observation can be quite profound, as Pauline Stafford shows:

> 'Most of our legal classifications [of the hierarchy of early medieval England] at this date are in royal document or laws, or produced by those anxious to define legal standing. It is scarcely surprising that most of them envisage a hierarchy in which relationship and service to the king are a major distinguishing criterion.'[34]

Given his position as one of the foremost political commentators on pre-Conquest England and the fact that several of his texts have served as a touchstone for those discussing the social hierarchy of the period, this section

---

[34] Stafford, *Unification and Conquest*, 151.

focuses on the oeuvre of Archbishop Wulfstan II of York. Thus, I reassess the famous *Geþyncðu* corpus (which places thegn and ceorl as distinct social categories), briefly exploring his use of the aforementioned Three Orders model and considering a previously uninterrogated binary model which places the *maga* (powerful) and *unmaga* (weak) in opposition, and revisit the *Rectitudines singularum personarum*, drawing out the latter's ideological underpinnings. All of this serves to illustrate that Wulfstan did not subscribe to one single, simple model to fully encapsulate the complexity of society. He altered his rhetoric and language choices to describe the inhabitants of early medieval England in line with the purpose of each work. This should influence our own approaches to describing the hierarchy of the period.

Thegns are, of course, just one part of the picture and many of the commentators discussed so far in this Element have focused on this group to the minimization of ceorls. This is, perhaps, quite a natural development given how many more sources discuss thegns instead of ceorls. Still, this is something that this final section seeks to redress, focusing on granular, dispositive documentation in order to supplement the work of Fleming, Senecal, and Williams and provide new case studies which shed further light on status-construction on the ground. Thus, Section 4 explores how these status- and rank-related complications manifested in local political landscapes, discussing a range of source-types, including charters, manumissions, and guild records. Together, these texts – which were not specifically created to advocate a particular world view – reveal the types of spaces and opportunities which facilitated the process of renegotiating hierarchical relations which occurred in early medieval England and point to a need for a robust language to describe inhabitants of early medieval England who moved through the realm's plastic social boundaries.

2 The Challenges of Describing Hierarchy

2.1 Introduction

Mapping the meaning of a word and, therefore, the meaning of a related identity is a daunting task. Indeed, the plasticity of language, and the liminal categories which can result from its use, has fascinated humans across the ages. One form in which the multivalency of words has garnered sustained attention is that of the riddle. A riddle, though typically crafted with one intended solution, often elicits a variety of responses. The fluidity of meaning proves to be the very crux of the contest. The challenge of unravelling an unexpected description of a subject proved a popular source of entertainment in early medieval England, as evidenced by the sizeable number of riddles which survive from the period. Even under the scrutiny of generations of scholars, many Old English riddles have refused to yield, with no consensus reached and the many solutions offered seeming as plausible as each other. For example, riddle seventy-four of the Exeter Book, only five short lines in length, has prompted at least thirteen wildly dissimilar answers: barnacle goose, boat, cuttlefish, figurehead, oak, quill pen, sea eagle, shadows, siren, soul, sun, swan, and water.[35] For the purposes of this section, this diversity of solutions highlights a fundamental problem which pervades our attempts to name the world around us: concepts, and the words associated with them, are highly plastic, or multivalent. The same bundle of words, arranged in the same order, can signify different – and sometimes irreconcilable – things to diverse people. For the historian seeking to impose order on the worlds of the past and to convey their understanding to others in the field, this offers a significant stumbling block.

This section will, therefore, build upon the three observations made by Christine Senecal (see Introduction) and problematise in greater detail the social boundary which lay between ceorl and thegn during the tenth and eleventh centuries. The scholarship which has emerged in the past two decades since Senecal's thoughts were put to paper is used to inform a new survey of the early English material that seemingly indicates what constituted a thegn. What is revealed is that there are almost no constants across our surviving sources which served to define who and what a thegn might be. Instead, a thegn seems to have connoted many things, but denoted little. Bringing this discussion of the primary sources into conversation with sociological and philosophical models which detail how concepts are constructed and communicated, a new approach to conceptualising what the rank of thegn signified to contemporaries is therefore posited. This produces a body of representational components which served to allow those in early medieval England (and scholars today) to identify who could conceivably claim thegnly rank. Having identified a more holistic and detailed understanding of how the rank of thegn worked, the latter half of the section considers two case studies of how scholars often describe the inhabitants of early medieval England and offers a potential solution for how we may better describe them and improve communication in the field.

2.2 Naming the Past

The philosophical works of Eleanor Rosch and her successors provide a different point of entry into thinking about the contradiction which arises when we, as scholars, attempt to define terms in our historical studies. Lexical concepts are complex entities associated with individual words, composed of

---

[35] Niles, 'Exeter Book Riddle 74'.

other concepts or representational components.[36] For clarity, let us begin with a simple example: a chair. We may define the lexical concept of the chair via the representational components of having four legs, a seat, and a back support. This traditional, definitional approach to constructing categories is remarkably old, stretching all the way back to Aristotelian philosophy. It is also, however, quite limited. There are many items of furniture that might come to mind which we could classify as a chair that do not fit such a strict definition. Try as we might, there is no one perfect definition. Even the *OED*'s best and most ambiguous effort – 'a seat for one person, typically movable, supported by four legs or feet, and having a rest for the back' – is not foolproof: first and foremost, how is an atypical chair different from a stool?[37] The definitional approach to lexical concepts is underpinned by an inherent and troublesome inflexibility.[38] The constituting factors named are either universal or they are not.[39] This implies that the answers we develop are either right or they are wrong.

Although elegant, the classical theory overlooks that, among philosophers, there is little agreement in defining even fundamental words. We might, therefore, turn to a probabilistic approach or prototype model, which allows that a 'bundle' of representational components defines a concept and that an object or person still aligns with the perception as long it demonstrates some of the components.[40] This allows us to build a wider base of representational components which constituted the concept of the chair, for instance. So, one might list

---

[36] Rosch, 'Cognitive Representations of Semantic Categories'. These components might well be conceptual rather than having any empirical basis, but, as Edouard Machery states, they are always treated as empirical truths, being revised only in light of 'empirical' discoveries; see Machery, 'A Better Philosophy for a Better Psychology', 94–95. On compound concepts, see Osherson and Smith, 'On the Adequacy of Prototype Theory'. For broader critique of Rosch's model, see Medin and Schaffer, 'Context Theory of Classification Learning'; Margolis and Laurence, *Concepts*.

[37] 'Chair, *N*. (1), Sense 2.a.', *Oxford English Dictionary* (Oxford University Press, 2023) [last accessed 20 June 2024] https://doi.org/10.1093/OED/7032493816.

[38] Machery, 'A Better Philosophy for a Better Psychology'.

[39] Taylor, *Linguistic Categorization*, 23.

[40] Machery, 'A Better Philosophy for a Better Psychology', 94–95. There is an alternative theory of how we develop categories, known as the exemplar theory, in which individuals possess an exemplar for a particular category. When an individual encounters new stimuli which may be judged against the exemplar, they are included or excluded based upon the number of similarities they share with the exemplar. Despite voracious scholarly disagreement regarding which of these two approaches is correct, more recent scholarship suggests that perhaps both the probabilistic/prototype and exemplar models are used by people to generate categories. They are simply employed in different situations. Whatever the case may be, the key is that the categories we use are not practically definitional and are able to encompass a variety of objects which lie across a spectrum in terms of their similarity to a prototype or exemplar. Indeed, this capacity for plasticity is one of the building blocks that allow for effective cognition, communication, and collective action. See Divjak and Arppe, 'Extracting Prototypes from Exemplars'.

that a chair is *likely* to be a seat for one person, have four legs, feature a back support, include armrests, and be made of a rigid material. There are more items that one could add to the list, but the key is that the probabilistic model allows that no item needs to fulfil all these aspects to be socially conceived as being a chair. If an item displays enough of these representational components, then we are able to identify it as a chair and, importantly, feel confident that another individual – even if their criteria differ somewhat – will still share a similar understanding. This is a fundamental aspect of human communication. As has been noted by George Lakoff, 'Without the ability to categorize, we could not function at all, either in the physical world or in our social and intellectual lives [and] an understanding of how we categorize is central to any understanding of how we think and how we function.'[41] Similarly, if we are to understand the social hierarchy of early medieval England, then we need to develop an approach that identifies the prototypes and/or exemplars (for which read the 'ideal') of key sociopolitical categories and that also accommodates the variation that permeates any such groupings.

Terms of representations such as 'thegn' and 'ceorl' first appear to denote specific social ranks. Indeed, the 'ideal' form of a thegn or ceorl can be found in certain cases. However, when we examine evidence from early medieval England more closely, what is revealed is a complex set of potential connotations, or opportunities of representation which are not fixed or constant. Thus, the problem just outlined affects fundamental objects of study more than one might think. The multivalency of social identifiers was not merely relegated to the margins of society and obscure terms – such as *fotsetla* – which appear only once in the extant Old English corpus, but also affected prevalent social terms – including *thegn* and *ceorl*.

Anyone who has studied early medieval England in any depth will have an idea of what constituted a thegn. It may look something like this: a noble-born warrior who was a retainer of a lord, held a manor of some five hides or so which was worked by freemen and slaves, and who was legally distinct from other ranks of society based upon their wergild (the compensation due for injury or murder).[42] This is, certainly, a popular conception, and there are reasonable grounds for such an image. Not only, as discussed in what follows, does the model of a five-hide thegn appear in the works of commentator Archbishop Wulfstan II of York, but there are archaeological examples of such estates, including the division of the sixty-hide estate of Shapwick, Somerset, into smaller five-hide parcels.[43] However, the problem with this definition quickly

---

[41] Lakoff, *Women, Fire, and Dangerous Things*, 5–6.
[42] For example, see O'Brien, 'Authority and Community', 86–87.
[43] Aston and Gerrard, *Interpreting the English Village*, 188–194.

becomes apparent. For example, the meaning of the term *thegn* changed over time, and before the tenth century it denoted a person who supplied service, while high rank was denoted by the word *gesith*. Thus, one might well argue that I should have described the thegn as a 'servant' instead of 'retainer'. After all, the word *thegn* can be translated either way and, even though the term *gesith* had largely fallen by the wayside in the tenth and eleventh centuries, service was still a fundamental part of thegnly identity.[44]

So, too, it is problematic to include the legal distinction of wergild. It would seem obvious to include the concept of a thegn being a *twelfhynde* (1,200 shillings) man given the many historians and students who have recited this as fact.[45] Yet, as Ann Williams points out, this legal division was less secure than one might think. Things were certainly unclear in this regard under King Cnut, who spoke to 'ealle mine þegnas twelfhynde 7 twihynde' (all my thegns, twelve-hundreders and two-hundreders).[46] In this instance, the legally separated categories of thegn and ceorl – allegedly rated at 1,200 and 200 shillings respectively – were brought together under the same designation of thegnly status. It may even be that such legal divisions were never explicitly tied to the rank of thegn except within a few minimally circulated documents.[47] Certainly, though the ninth-century Laws of Alfred divided the population into those with a wergild of *twihynde* (200), *syxhynde* (600), and *twelfhynde* (1,200) shillings, it only draws a clear connection between the rank of ceorl and the lowest level of legal compensation. The middling category disappeared from the written record in the tenth century, and it remains unclear to whom it referred.[48] Whatever the case may be, thegnliness was not necessarily directly equated with legal status. It may have operated alongside such legal divisions, and, in many cases, the rank of thegn might have indicated an individual's expected legal rights, but the relationship between these two was fluid.

Even as early as the first half of the tenth century, the term *thegn* seems to be used in a rather nebulous manner. Preserved as a Latin translation in the twelfth-century text known as *Quadripartitus*, a Kentish ratification of the laws of tenth-century King Æthelstan addresses 'omnes Cantescyrae thaini, comites et villani'.[49] Given that *comes* could be interpreted to denote a thegn, Williams understandably translates this as 'all the thegns of Kent, thegns and ceorls'.[50] Still, the framing is remarkably reminiscent of the recurrent Old English

---

[44] Loyn, 'Gesith and Thegns'.

[45] For example, see Wormald, 'Anglo-Saxon Law and Scots Law', 195–196.   [46] S 985.

[47] Sukhino-Khomenko, '"Thrymsa, a Coin [Not] in Circulation in Northern England"'. On wergild, see Oliver, 'Wergild, Mund, and Manbot'.

[48] Williams, *The World before Domesday*, 1.   [49] III at Preface.

[50] Williams, *The World before Domesday*, 8.

rhetorical device of contrasting eorl with ceorl.[51] In the Laws of Alfred, treason was discussed in relation to 'be eallum hadum, ge ceorle ge eorle' (all ranks, either ceorl or eorl).[52] Another text issued during Æthelstan's reign and similarly preserved in *Quadripartitus*, the ordinances of a London peace-guild (*frið-gyld*), notes that the membership was comprised of 'ægðen ge eorlisce ge ceorlisce' (both eorlish and ceorlish) individuals.[53] From King Edmund's reign, we find the Latin formulation appear once again: 'comes uel uillanus'.[54] However, here it is juxtaposed with 'prepositus uel tainus' (reeve or thegn). *Comes*, therefore, does not seem to have indicated thegnliness but, rather, a sense of nobility, at least in the middle of the tenth century, while the title of thegn denoted a particular form of service.[55]

At the beginning of the eleventh century, Archbishop Wulfstan remarked that each rank, 'ge eorl ge ceorl, ge þegen ge þeoden' (whether eorl or ceorl, thegn or lord), was entitled to the appropriate honour.[56] It may be, as Stefan Jurasinski and Lisi Oliver have suggested, that the juxtaposition of eorl and ceorl is simply 'a frozen formulaic expression here meaning "all free men"'.[57] Such a reading, while plausible for some instances where it is deployed, would see this turn of phrase rendered somewhat redundant in Æthelstan's early tenth-century address to the thegns of Kent. If holding the rank of thegn, surely it would be needless to note that they were free from bondage. Whether rendered as *comites et villani* or *eorl ge ceorl*, this phrase points towards a sense of social stratification along the lines of something other than legal distinction. That something is probably the division between noble and non-noble.[58] Thus, the royal address to both noble and non-noble Kentish thegns provides an earlier counterpart to that of Cnut's greeting to his twelve-hundreder and two-hundreder thegns. The relationship between rank, function, legal status, and noble condition had, therefore, long been far from linear in tenth- and eleventh-century England.

To further illustrate the complicated relationship between these factors, it is worth interrogating the idea of nobility in more detail. Discussing medieval Europe, Timothy Reuter defines the nobility as a group whose status was defined legally. For those who exercised 'power as a result of being well-born in a socially rather than legally defined sense', he favours the term *aristocrat*.[59]

---

[51] Something noted also by George Molyneaux. See Molyneaux, 'The *Ordinance concerning the Dunsæte*', 266.

[52] Af 4.2.   [53] Liebermann, *Die Gesetze der Angelsachsen*, 173.   [54] III Em. 7.2.

[55] Molyneaux, 'The *Ordinance concerning the Dunsæte*', 266–267.

[56] Liebermann, *Die Gesetze der Angelsachsen*, 456–458.

[57] Jurasinski and Oliver, *The Laws of Alfred*, 295.

[58] Andrew Rabin offers a similar interpretation, translating '*eorl ge ceorl*' as 'noble and layman'. See Rabin, *The Political Writings of Archbishop Wulfstan of York*, 68.

[59] Reuter, 'The Medieval Nobility in Twentieth Century Historiography', 197.

In light of this, one might argue that the address made by Æthelstan to his thegns, *comites* and *villani* could be better rendered as 'aristocrat and non-aristocrat'.[60] The term *aristocrat* or *aristocracy*, however, comes accompanied with its own baggage from early modernity and the Latin word *nobilis* was, at least, used in early English documents. Rachel Stone raises some further problems that arise from Reuter's neat division, observing that it 'leaves unanswered both what counts as exercising power, and the position of particular women, monks or children who did not directly wield power, but whom the sources nevertheless call *nobilis*'.[61] I will, therefore, not be using the term *aristocrat* here. For the purposes of this discussion, I will continue to use the word *noble* (and, conversely, *non-noble*) to describe thegns who are well-born (or not), the distinctions between which will be teased out later in this Element. This allows us to uncouple the term *thegn*, in line with the evidence from the period, from both legal and lineage-derived standing, opening the door to a more nuanced interpretation of the various ways in which thegnliness could be performed and deployed.

Two mainstays of the characteristics which were used in the Middle Ages to qualify the nobility of an individual were conduct and descent.[62] This appears to be true in early medieval England. Surviving ecclesiastical sources do seem to have sought to instil qualities such as camaraderie, loyalty to companions, urbane eloquence, and gentleness (*mansuetudo*) among the ruling elites.[63] The oppositional vices of wrathfulness and vengefulness had the potential to embroil local societies and social groups in destructive networks of conflict. Thus, elites were encouraged to be slow to anger, not to seek revenge, and to tolerate immediate wrongs for the sake of a more distant goal. For a group whose serried ranks dominated the judicial sphere, wisdom and honesty were necessarily paramount virtues. Concerning issues of descent, the Old English corpus provides various words in which the nobility of someone's heritage is indicated, such as *æþelboren* (noble-born) and *gesiðcundes* (*gesith*-born).[64]

The link between nobility and thegnliness is rather complex. A little-discussed late tenth-century law code concerning grave robbery – titled by

---

[60] The terms *aristocrat* and *aristocracy* were particularly popular in the decades around the year 2000, but they have enjoyed consistent usage since. For example, see Fleming, 'The New Wealth'; Senecal, 'Keeping up with the Godwinesons'; Crouch, *The English Aristocracy*; Williams, *The World before Domesday*; Moilanen, 'The Concept of the Three Orders', 1331–1352; Coss, *The Aristocracy in England and Tuscany*.

[61] Stone, *Morality and Masculinity*, 24.   [62] Crouch, *The Birth of Nobility*, 29–86, 124–155.

[63] Gillingham, 'Thegns and Knights', 144–150.

[64] *Æþelboren* is found mainly in homiletic material of the tenth and eleventh centuries, but it does appear in chronicles also. See Bosworth, *An Anglo-Saxon Dictionary*, 22. *Gesiðcundes* enjoyed more consistent usage earlier in the period – for example, the Laws of Ine. See Ine 46; Loyn, 'Gesith and Thegns'; Bosworth, *An Anglo-Saxon Dictionary*, 413.

modern scholars as the *Walreaf* – illustrates the social importance of familial descent for thegns: 'Walre is niðinges dæde. Gif hwa of sacenwille, do þæt mid eahta 7 feowertig fulborenra þegena' (Corpse robbery is an outlaw's deed. If someone should wish to be acquitted, [they should] do so with forty-eight full-born thegns).[65] Regardless of how widely such an unusual law was ever put into practice, the code suggests that it was possible to conceptualise difference within the thegnhood based on ancestry. A full-born thegn – presumably someone whose parents (or perhaps parents and grandparents) were thegns – was more prestigious than a person who achieved the rank of thegn but did not have the correct familial past. The *Ordinance concerning the Dunsǽte*, arguably issued in the late tenth or early eleventh century, centres the hereditary distinction between thegns and ceorls, contrasting 'þegenboren' (thegn-born) with 'ceorlboren' (ceorl-born).[66] Wulfstan's *Norðleoda laga* reinforces the notion that the attainment of thegnly rank was envisaged as ennobling an individual's lineage. Still, the use of *gesiðcundes* to describe the noble lineage they will acquire after several generations perhaps implies that these two qualities, while related, are not synonymous. Drawing these sources together, one could perhaps say that there were: those who were ceorl-born and still ceorls; those who were ceorl-born and gained the prestige of being thegnly yet remained non-noble; and those who were born thegns and were, therefore, noble. In short, there could be a hereditary element to thegnliness yet there was also another division within the thegnage based upon lineage. This might explain why Æthelstan referred to his noble and non-noble thegns.

This survey of nobility in the period is not comprehensive, but it does highlight a variable relationship between the ideas of nobleness and thegnliness. A simpler explanation may simply be that these inconsistencies result from the differing understandings of the various authors. The often-cited example of a seventh-century king's thegn called Imma draws out the importance of comportment as a means of social differentiation. So ingrained were Imma's noble qualities, according to Bede, that, even when he tried to hide his rank by pretending to be a peasant during his captivity, his 'appearance, his bearing, and his speech' revealed his standing.[67] This seems to draw a firmer connection between thegnliness and noble conduct. Of course, this account, though reworked in the tenth century by Ælfric, may not tell us much about the practicalities of being 'noble' in late tenth- and eleventh-century England. We do know that thegns were often expected to be pious and, ideally, generous

---

[65] Liebermann, *Die Gesetze der Angelsachsen*, 392.

[66] Molyneaux, 'The *Ordinance concerning the Dunsǽte*', 267.

[67] Colgrave and Mynors, ed. and trans., *Bede's Ecclesiastical History of the English People*, 400–405.

patrons of the Church. Aspects of these thegnly qualities were often demonstrated through pastimes, such as hunting, or through the sponsoring of a local religious institution.[68] These sorts of activities are certainly what we would expect to see from those seeking to demonstrate their nobility. However, the two, while often linked, do not seem to have been necessarily synonymous. All nobles may have been thegns, but not all thegns were noble. Moreover, a thegn or ceorl in the heartlands of Wessex may well have exhibited nobility somewhat differently than their counterparts in Cornwall, the Welsh Marches, the East Midlands, or Northumbria. It is also worth bearing in mind the caveat that accompanies any such exclusionary behaviours: anyone, if armed with the right resources, can adopt such behaviours and make use of them as part of their social repertoire.

Returning to how we might define the term *thegn* as a term of representation, a thegn might be labelled a 'warrior', a 'retainer', a 'servant', 'free', a '1,200' man', and a 'juror'. To this list we might add 'noble', 'powerful', and 'lord'. Ownership of physical objects could also form part of these representational components: 'land' or to be 'landed'; military accoutrements, including a 'coat (of mail)', 'shield', 'spear', 'sword', and a 'horse'; and to be 'wealthy'. We might also include what has been termed the *trinoda necessitas*, the three obligations of military service, maintenance of fortresses, and work on bridges. Many more aspects might still be added to this list, such as *scipe* or five hides, or arguably removed. Regardless, even with this relatively modest list of representational components it would not be hard to find examples of thegns who did not fulfil these criteria. Issues arise when we envisage that each thegn fulfilled all of these criteria. At the loosest end of the definitional spectrum, Jake Stattel offers the possibility that the term *thegn* 'was simply used as a legal term for any landowner of a certain social and possibly military calibre, even relatively poor individuals'.[69] Moreover, the term *thegn* was perhaps applied more liberally in the Danelaw than elsewhere, so much so that free Scandinavian newcomers who had settled in the region could call themselves thegns without causing controversy.[70] Speaking of what comprised an English noble after the Conquest, David Crouch provides a rather neat definition: 'a man who dressed and acted like a nobleman and was not laughed at'.[71] This works just as well, I should think, for the early medieval period and the task of defining a thegn. Anyone who could claim the rank of thegn without facing contestation was treated as

---

[68] On hunting practices see Flight, 'Aristocratic Deer Hunting in Late Anglo-Saxon England'. On the founding of churches, see Higham, 'The Godwins, Towns and St Olaf Churches'.

[69] Stattel, 'Legal Culture in the Danelaw', 201.

[70] Stattel, 'Legal Culture in the Danelaw', 200–201. See also Day, 'Sokemen and Freemen'.

[71] Crouch, *The Birth of Nobility*, 3.

a thegn. As John Blair succinctly frames the matter: 'the best way to become a thegn may well have been to behave like one: to be brave and generous, to display conspicuous wealth, to spend it lavishly'.[72] Perhaps the most productive path forward is to consider the representational components already outlined and to assume that an individual considered thegnly was likely able to perform several of these attributes, both displaying various material acquisitions and participating in commensurate social functions.

It should, at this juncture, be quite evident that if one turns to the term *ceorl*, such issues continue to dog our efforts for terminological clarity. Williams highlights such difficulties in her contemplation of the problems which manifest through translation:

> The only thing which all ceorls had in common was that legally they were neither thegns nor slaves. It is for this reason that *ceorl* is better translated as 'free man' rather than as 'peasant', for not only has the latter acquired pejorative associations, but it is also clear that not all *ceorlas* personally worked the land; some were themselves landlords with dependants who worked it for them.[73]

One might argue, given the slew of conflicting evidence relating to the legal standing of thegns in the period, that the word *legally* might be better replaced by the word *socially* in Williams's definition. We return to the idea that the term *ceorl* indicated little more about the person to whom it was applied than that they were not of noble stock.[74] In short, ceorls could be many things in many circumstances to many people. They could be subsistence farmers, swineherds, artisans, itinerant labourers, officers, and even lords. While some ceorls might be denied the right to possess a weapon, for others, such as the *geneat* or the *cnihtas*, it seems to have been necessary to the completion of their activities. We could even make a good argument that they could not necessarily be defined by their freedom. As Dominique Barthélemy and Alice Rio have persuasively argued, freedom was, in practice, a spectrum ranging from the unfree, to the semi-free, through to the free. Of the unfree, the late Paul Hyams stated that, even within this legal category, experiences ranged from 'the unbearably harsh ... to a milder subordination'.[75] In some ways, the task of defining a ceorl presents an even greater mountain to climb. One could compile a list of representational components associated with the concept of ceorlishness that dwarf those associated with the rank of thegn. Thus, there is a suite of components that gives shape to an idea of a generic ceorl which allows (and allowed)

---

[72] Blair, *Building*, 377.   [73] Williams, *The World before Domesday*, 2.
[74] Richard Abels favoured such a broad definition in Abels, *Lordship and Military Obligation*, 37–42.
[75] Hyams, 'Servitude', 129–130.

a loose identification of such individuals, but it is always contextual and ill-defined when taken as a whole. The plasticity of these social identifiers produces a situation in which we can see representational components that stretch across both the social categories of thegn and ceorl.

2.3 Alternative Models of Hierarchy

Terms such as *ceorl* and *thegn* provide a general sense of someone's position in society and, often, the way they sustained their lifestyle, but they do not necessarily best convey a sense of the dynamics of the power wielded within vertical relations. In short, the labels of 'ceorl' and 'thegn' are not necessarily as useful or precise as one might wish. Approaching the problem of studying medieval hierarchies and to capture a sense of the forces which produced and maintained structures of inequality, historians have developed other ways of describing the inhabitants of the Middle Ages, including through models derived from the works of late nineteenth- and early twentieth-century thinkers Karl Marx and Max Weber. Marx divided society into classes, viewing vertical relations through the lens of labour. Though dominating early analyses, this was largely superseded by the 'liberal' stratification theory in the latter half of the twentieth century. Channelling the Weberian-inspired 'trinity of inequalities' – wealth, power, and status – American stratification theorists, such as Robert Nisbet, embraced status, rather than class, as the key vector by which society is divided.[76] Thus, the role of social prestige, rather than economic relations, became much more important in such readings. Though these two approaches have spawned a myriad of ways in which scholars conceptualise and describe the hierarchy of English society in the period, for the sake of brevity, I will detail just two. The first approach frames early medieval society in terms of peasants and landholders or lords, and the second divides the inhabitants of England into lords and their dependants.[77]

The word *peasant* has long been deployed by students of the past to refer to those who worked the land. Though the term is nowhere to be found within the period in question, it does originate in the Middle Ages. Derived from the Old French *païsant*, it came in Middle English (*paisaunt*) to denote someone who was not noble and laboured in the countryside.[78] Although a word which has been used in many different scholarly paradigms, it has widely been used to frame modes of extraction through the lens of labour. For those writing in a Marxian or historical materialist framework (and even those writing in

---

[76] Rigby, *English Society in the Later Middle Ages*, 6.

[77] Other forms of dividing early English society include lord/tenant or free/unfree.

[78] 'Paisaunt n.', *MED*.

response), *peasant* and *lord* are terms which speak to individuals' economic roles. Therefore, these terms represent different 'classes' or, to be more faithful to the work of Marx and Engels, 'estates'.[79] Given the centrality of the desire to maximise income in historical materialism, peasants and lords were seen as inherently and perpetually existing in a state of conflict, the division marked along (theoretically) clear economic lines. Here, the economic base (defined by relations and means of production) informs the superstructure (in short, everything else). The idea of the 'community' of peasant society and the tendency to treat the peasantry as a homogenous entity has rightly received sustained critique.[80] Historians of later medieval society, such as Miri Rubin and Stephen Rigby, have pointed out the heterogeneity of such societies.[81] Even the eminent Marxist historian Rodney Hilton acknowledged that tension and inequality existed in the peasant strata.[82] Today, few remain wedded to such a rigid, economic definition of the peasant or peasantry, and the label 'peasant' is widely utilised in a generous manner by many scholars, accompanied by an implicit acceptance that such imprecise use of the word is largely necessary.

Still, it is hard to get away from the sense that the word *peasant* indicates a form of labour, one that was commonly performed at a lord's behest. This, of course, poses some problems when looking to early medieval England. We might struggle to justify calling the very top of the ceorlish stratum peasants. As noted, some were landholders in their own right with a sizeable body of workers who laboured on their land, thus blurring the boundary between 'peasant' and 'lord'. Moreover, those who were of ceorlish rank but earned their livelihood through trade or through an occupation (such as smithing or carpentry) might also, arguably, not be best understood as either peasants or lords. Thus, the lord–peasant framework, though serving to uncover informative aspects about the economic relations (and some aspects of social relations) of this world, often unintentionally elides key social differences within these local landscapes. It is perhaps at its most useful when interrogating the creation of social hierarchy through the lens of economic activity and thus capturing a sense of potential flashpoints which arise through the exploitation of labour, though even in such instances it is sensible to proceed with caution.

By comparison, the lord–dependant model attempts to represent vertical relationships through the cultivation of dependency, particularly along legal and tenurial vectors. Though the word *dependant* may be applied to anyone, of any rank, who was obligated to serve a lord, it has become synonymous with

---

[79] Rigby, 'Historical Materialism, Social Structure, and Social Change in the Middle Ages'.
[80] Schofield, *Peasant and Community in Medieval England*, 5–6.
[81] Rubin, 'Small Groups', 134; Rigby, *English Society in the Later Middle Ages*.
[82] Hilton, 'Reasons for Inequality among Medieval Peasants'.

non-noble laypeople. Even some of the most careful and nuanced readings of the lordly exercise of power and subjugation of the lower ranks of society have framed these relations according to this binary. It is not hard to see why: the less powerful might depend upon the lord in certain ways, such as the right to rent land, to leave his service, or to access justice. Seeing how lords coerced and shaped the lives of those within their reach, scholars have come to commonly depict these relations as between 'lords' and 'dependants'. A key reason for the adoption of the word *dependant* to describe subordinated members of society might be, as Alice Rio notes, that 'Since free/unfree corresponded to an earlier system of description which had originated in a very different society from that of the early middle ages, social historians have tended to place greater trust in the couple lord/dependant as representing early medieval relations of power and production, and to abandon free/unfree to historians of law.'[83] In a bid to ensure that they did not 'anachronistically' use a method of social delineation from the late antique period, historians of early medieval Europe embraced an alternative framework which 'represented society as a sliding scale of hierarchical, bilateral ties of lordship and dependence'.[84] Given that relationality and intersubjectivity are key when trying to understand the manifestation and constitution of status, centring the dependence that a lord can inculcate among his followers can be beneficial.[85]

Still, an example taken from the oeuvre of the eminent Paul Hyams highlights some of the risks which arise when using this framework: 'I use the word "lord" throughout for anyone who enjoys lordship over *dependents*, including possible slaves.'[86] Hyams's work commonly displays a nuanced understanding of the application of power in early medieval England and frames subordination as a 'spectrum'.[87] His use of *dependant* – which operates in this context as an homogenising term – thus seems to lie at odds with his purposes. After the fashion of Rio – who suggests that the free–unfree binary has misled historians and that 'grey-area' statuses were not only present but also, occasionally, desired – I, too, argue that the lord–dependant framework presents an often unhelpful binary.[88] It captures a sense of the relationality of power but flattens the degrees of difference between individuals' experience, especially in cases where *dependant* is used to refer to anyone from the lower strata of society. I have made the case elsewhere that this is neither a productive nor an ethical

---

[83] Rio, '"Half-Free" Categories', 130.   [84] Rio, '"Half-Free" Categories', 129.

[85] Pracy, '"Medeman Mannum"', 54–78. See also Hyams, 'Servitude', 132.

[86] Hyams, 'Servitude', 130. Italics my own, for emphasis. Note the American English spelling of the word 'dependant'.

[87] Hyams, 'Servitude', 130.

[88] Rio, '"Half-Free" Categories', 130. See also Barthélemy, *The Serf*, 51–65.

way of framing the lives of those who dwelt in the landscape of early medieval England. However, that is all I will say on this matter, for this is not the venue for such discussion.

For the purposes of this section, what is vital is that a lord or dependent in this model could theoretically occupy an array of different social positions. The slave, swineherd, baker, trader, carpenter, smith, wet nurse, wealthy geneat, and thegn could, according to such a model, be seen as dependants. All would be brought under the homogenising term *dependant*, despite each having a different capacity to influence their personal circumstances. The geneat, merchant, thegn, king's thegn, and ealdorman might all be identifiable as a lord within this framework. Yet the gulf in power and self-determination enjoyed by geneat and ealdorman was large. Thus, though it can help capture the relationality of a form of power and, when discussing specific instances, may offer some utility, in discussing the broader swathes of social relations it often omits important social gradations.

Neither model represents a 'silver bullet' to solving the complexities of these social entanglements nor supersedes usage of terminology from the period. Rather, all can be used in conjunction with each other to generate a more specific image of the period. When treated as part of a larger toolkit, the possibility of a more nuanced understanding of early English society – especially the lower strata – becomes increasingly realisable. There is, of course, the tension that arises from wishing to engage deeply with the granular data which survives from the period and attempting to draw out wider narratives. Hilton, writing in 1974, summed this issue up well, stating that 'any serious historian has to classify and generalise social phenomena', but that historians' 'oversimplifications of the stages of history' present a persistent danger.[89] It seems to me that the most productive path is to embrace the plasticity of social boundaries and pinpoint social actors along relevant communal and political vectors. Thus, we might identify an individual as a member of the ceorlish peasantry, the dependant thegnhood, the lordly ceorls, or the unfree peasantry. Even this approach homogenises these people more than one would like, and, in many circumstances, it would be best practice to frame the social position of historic inhabitants of early medieval England in relation to their rank, class, occupation, legal status, tenurial situation, ability to access resources, and, among others, affect change in the local discourse of power. This is not always a practicable option in many studies. Academic writing, while necessitating specificity, demands both clarity and brevity. Nonetheless, it is imperative that we remain aware of the multivalency of the terms used by those who documented the world around them in the past and the 'flattening' nature of the tools

---

[89] Hilton, 'Medieval Peasants: Any Lessons?'

we use as historians. Even when we look to the period, we find not just one way of thinking about hierarchy, but rather, as seen in Section 3, the signs of an early medieval sociological 'toolkit'.

3 Early Medieval Visions of Social Hierarchy

3.1 Introduction

It should come as no surprise that our scholarly attempts to model the hierarchy of pre-Conquest England are best served by using the compound method posited earlier in this Element, especially since, as this section will show, even early medieval commentators did not favour a one-size-fits-all approach. Vertical relations were represented using a variety of different lenses in the period, each chosen according to the specific need of the author. Given the need for brevity, Archbishop Wulfstan II of York (r. 1002–d. 1023) will serve as the case study for this section. This choice is, of course, by no means arbitrary. Wulfstan authored or edited many texts which describe the hierarchy of tenth- and eleventh-century England and, given his role in the successive regimes of Kings Æthelred II and Cnut, was well positioned to be one of the foremost political commentators of the period. While this section cannot provide a comprehensive analysis of Wulfstan's entire corpus (other scholars – such as Dorothy Bethurum and Andrew Rabin – have already admirably performed such a task), four key texts/body of texts will be discussed: the *Geþyncðu* corpus and the so-called promotion law; his discussion of the Three Orders model in *The Institutes of Polity*; his previously undiscussed articulation of a binary between the *maga* (strong) and *unmaga* (weak) in the law code of Æthelred; and, finally, his amendments to the *Rectitudines singularum personarum*, a treatise discussing estate management.[90] All these texts bear the traces of Wulfstan's influence and his desire to forge a 'holy society'. Each text seeks to regulate and remould the behaviour of the populace of England in a more 'moral' fashion, but Wulfstan utilised distinctly differing lenses by which to describe the society which surrounded him. In short, the ideas of thegn and ceorl served to reflect one type of relationship and a way of conceptualising early English society. They were not all-encompassing terms and Wulfstan was forced to make use of a wider lexicon to better capture the complexities of the society of early medieval England. This, I suggest, should inform our own endeavours to describe the hierarchy of the polity in question and, hence, utilise a compound methodology.

---

[90] Among many other publications, see Bethurum, 'Archbishop Wulfstan's Commonplace Book', 916–929; Bethurum, *The Homilies of Wulfstan*; Rabin, *The Political Writings of Archbishop Wulfstan of York*; Rabin, *Archbishop Wulfstan of York: Old English Legal Writings*.

3.2 Wulfstan and *Geþyncðu*

Two texts composed by Wulfstan in the early eleventh century, *Geþyncðu* (*Promotion Law*) and *Norðleoda laga* (*Laws of the Northumbrians*), have long lain at the heart of academic conceptions of what defined thegnliness and ceorlishness.[91] It is not hard to see why, as the texts provide the only explicit descriptions of how someone might move from one rank to the other. *Geþyncðu* famously describes how each rank was entitled to the appropriate honour:

> Hit wæs hwilum on Engla lagum, þæt leod 7 agu for be geþinðum; 7 þa wæron leod witan weorðscipes wyrðe, æle be his mæðe, eorl ge ceorl, þegen ge þeoden. 7 gif ceorl gefeah, þæt he hæfde fullice fif hida agenes landes, cirican 7 kyeenan, bellhus 7 burhgeat, setl 7 sundernote on cynges healle, þonne wæs he þanon forð þegenrihtes weorðe.

> § 1 In the laws of the English, it once was that people and law were ordered by rank;[92] and the people's councillors were treated with dignity, each according to his rank, eorl and ceorl,[93] thegn and lord.

> § 2 And if a ceorl prospered so that he had fully five hides of his own property with a church and kitchen, a bell-house and fortified gate, a seat and an appointed role in the king's hall, then he was worthy of a thegn's rights ever after.[94]

Featuring a particularly striking caveat, *Norðleoda laga* presents perhaps one of the most quoted passages on Anglo-Saxon society:

> Gif ceorlisc man ge-þeo þæt he hæbbe v hida landes to cynges utware, 7 man hine ofslea, forgylde man hine mid ii þusend þrymsa. þeh he geþeo þæt he hæbbe helm 7 byrnan, 7 goldfæted sweord, gif he þæt land nafaþ, he byþ ceorl swa þeah. gif his sunu 7 his suna sunu þæt geþeoð, þæt hy swa micel landes habbað, syððan byþ se ofspring gesiðcundes cynnes, be twam ðusendum þrymsa. 7 gif hig þæt nabbað ne to þam geþeon ne magan, gylde man cyrlisce

> § 9 And if a ceorlish man[95] prospers so that he has five hides of land for his obligations to the king and anyone kills him, compensation for him shall be two thousand thrymsas.

> § 10 Yet, even if he prospers so that he possesses a helmet and a coat of mail and a gold-plated sword, if he does not possess the land, he will still be ceorl.

---

[91] These texts still act as a touchstone for some academics. For example, see Lavelle, *Alfred's Wars*, 55.

[92] For the most part, I have followed Andrew Rabin's translation (Rabin, *The Political Writings of Archbishop Wulfstan of York*, 68–69). However, there are a few key areas that I have deemed it necessary to alter.

[93] See the earlier discussion in this Element regarding this turn of phrase.

[94] Liebermann, *Die Gesetze der Angelsachsen*, 456.

[95] Again, for the most part, I have followed Andrew Rabin's translation (Rabin, *The Political Writings of Archbishop Wulfstan of York*, 71). Nonetheless, I have made a few alterations. I have favoured a more literal translation of 'ceorlisc man'.

§ 11 And if his son and his son's son prosper so that they have sufficient land, then the offspring will be of gesith-born kin at [a wergild of] two thousand thrymsas.

§ 12 And if they do not have and cannot acquire enough, their compensation will be that of a ceorl.[96]

Despite the seemingly plausible regulations and pathway to social advancement laid out by Wulfstan, academic treatments of these texts have grown increasingly sceptical.[97] Whereas once they were taken to be representative of normative social boundaries, the nostalgic tone and the lack of any corroboration for these practices elsewhere has prompted historians to handle them with care.

Forming part of a larger compilation on society and social order, including *Mircna laga* (*Laws of the Mercians*), *Að* (*Oath*), and *Hadbot* (*Compensation for the Ordained*), the *Geþyncðu* group were not official documents in the same way that we may think of early English law codes or writs. Rather, they seem to have enjoyed only a limited degree of circulation and were recorded in manuscripts which contained material that Wulfstan referenced when drafting later law codes. The collection, at all points, retains its focus on dividing ranks across society and ensuring conformity. *Mircna laga* describes the wergild of a ceorl, a thegn, and a king according to an alleged Mercian tradition, while *Að* rounds out the picture of the relative worth of a ceorl to a thegn, stipulating that the wergild of a thegn was six times that of a ceorl.[98] Furthermore, *Að* distinctly draws out that the ranks of a mass-priest and a thegn were equivalent in the eyes of the compiler. Lastly, the *Hadbot*, as a means to protect and safeguard the clergy, lays out the levels of compensation to be paid if anyone transgressed against a member of the Church.

Though it has often been held that there was some ninth-century core to these texts (in particular, the first half of *Norðleoda laga*, *Mircna laga*, and the first clause of *Að*), it may be that even this was not the case.[99] Thus, the corpus seems little more than Wulfstan's personal attempt to conjure order during a period which was witness to an increasingly fraught and confused system of day-to-day social classification. At the very least, it is hard to imagine how the practicalities of these texts would ever have been implemented. How did those ceorls who were temporarily elevated operate within society? Before finally granting permanent elevation, who checked aspirants' assets to ensure

---

[96] For variations in the text recorded in CCCC MS 201 (D), *Textus Roffensis*, and *Quadripartitus*, see Liebermann, *Die Gesetze der Angelsachsen*, 458–461.

[97] For examples, see Lawson, *Cnut*, 60; Hadley, *The Northern Danelaw*, 74–75.

[98] Whitelock, *EHD I*, 433.

[99] Rabin, *The Political Writings of Archbishop Wulfstan of York*, 65; Sukhino-Khomenko, "'Thrymsa, a Coin [Not] in Circulation in Northern England'", 8–41.

they complied with the requisite qualifications? And what happened to those thegns who fell below the five-hide threshold? Unlike the practice of manumission – a ceremony which saw the emancipation of a slave – elevation to thegnly status was not marked by charter. Presumably this was because the act of manumitting involved the de-commodification of a person, arguably a more profound transition than moving up through society. Without a document to mark such movements, we must conclude it would have relied, as with many things in the period, upon communal remembering. In early medieval England, communities gathered together, acted as witnesses to important events and ceremonies, and remembered. Nevertheless, memory is not static, and social actors rely heavily on signifiers that indicate their place in society, as discussed in Section 2. Even those freed from slavery, whose new status was presumably marked by a charter which laid plain their rights, do not appear to have been safe from challenges to their status.[100] In short, the *Geþyncðu* group offers us limited insight into the actual workings of hierarchy in the period. As Rabin eloquently puts it, the corpus does 'not so much record defunct regional legal practices as it conjures a nostalgic image of an idealised past'.[101] Still, it does permit a compelling window into one of the ways Wulfstan chose to envision the society around him.

Unlike the Three Orders model, discussed later in this Element, which centres on the social function of certain groups, the *Geþyncðu* text focuses upon issues of rank. The rank of the thegn, in this accounting, is not justified by martial prowess. It is a thegn's tenurial status that affects their position in society. The ceorl who acquired and retained control over five hides was worthy of thegnly rank. Neither their liquid capital nor any martial service they performed, in Wulfstan's framework, was enough to warrant the promotion of a ceorl to thegnhood. It is in this attempt to outline what defined a thegn that Wulfstan sought to tie landed assets and rank more closely together, re-establishing what we may presume was a fading linkage. This whole tract can be read as an attempt to shore up certain social distinctions. What we are left with is a compelling image of an ordered English society, a text brimming with verisimilitude. Yet it was a corpus of ambitious prescriptive texts, seeking to refashion the social hierarchy in a more structured form. At best, it was loosely inspired by earlier texts and did not make it much beyond his private collection. The key, however, is not how *representative* it was, but rather that it was one method that Wulfstan utilised to make sense of the world which he inhabited.

---

[100] For example, see the case of Putrael and Ælfric, the man who tried to enslave him (Whitelock, *EHD I*, 562).

[101] Rabin, *The Political Writings of Archbishop Wulfstan of York*, 67.

And, for the purposes of these tracts, it was the binary of ceorl and thegn that served his authorial needs.

3.3 Revisiting the Three Orders

It may seem somewhat odd to revisit ground as well trodden as the ternary or tripartite model of society known as the Three Orders. Its use across Europe has been treated in detail and, even concerning the deployment of the model in early medieval England alone, both Timothy Powell and Inka Moilanen have given comprehensive analyses.[102] Yet, for all the nuances present in these earlier studies, one rather fundamental aspect is generally overlooked: that the rank of thegn and ceorl is not always mapped directly onto the roles of *bellatores* and *laboratores*. Powell took this model, at its most basic level, as one that divided society into the clergy, nobility, and peasantry. The first appearance of the Three Orders model in England is in an Old English translation of Boethius's *Consolation of Philosophy* (880 × 950) attributed to King Alfred. In this translation, it is declared that a king 'sceal habban gebedmen and fyrdmen and weorcmen' (must have praying men, fighting men, and working men). These are, according to the text, 'þrim geferscipum biwiste' (the three orders/ associations of men).[103] They are defined by functionality rather than rank. Indeed, Powell observed that it was 'more than a synthesis of the bipartite differentiation of clergy and laity with the bipartite stratification of nobles and peasants'.[104] This assertion was prompted because the model did not place these orders in a hierarchical structure as did the 'idea of the Three Estates of Clergy, Aristocracy and Commoners seen in France in 1789'.[105] For Powell, while the building blocks were similar, the manner of their depiction was more nuanced in this antecedent formulation. Inka Moilanen is more explicit in her inference that the *bellatores* were the 'secular aristocracy', whose purpose included 'military defence, the assurance of justice and the order of society'.[106] There is good reason for Moilanen's conclusion if one focuses on Ælfric's rendition of the ternary model. Expanding upon the tripartite divisions of society, Ælfric critiques the *bellatores* and states that a warrior who punishes evildoers is 'Godes þe[g]n'.[107] Thus, a connection is drawn between *bellatores*, thegnliness, and, in particular, ruling. That the *bellatores* were often read as referring to the thegnhood is thus a reasonable assumption. Nonetheless, the decision to focus upon the functionality of these groups demonstrates an awareness that these facets of

---

[102] Powell, 'The "Three-Orders"', 103–132; Moilanen, 'Society and Social Mobility', 1331–1352.

[103] Powell, 'The "Three-Orders"', 103.   [104] Powell, 'The "Three-Orders"', 104.

[105] Powell, 'The "Three-Orders"', 104.   [106] Moilanen, 'Society and Social Mobility', 1344.

[107] Moilanen, 'Society and Social Mobility', 1343.

status were divisible. Neither the rank nor relative dependency of the groups in question is stressed in these models. Rather, it is what we might describe as their class: the *laboratores* produce food and can be securely identified as peasants; the *bellatores* and *oratores*, given that their labour is directed to other ends and thus must benefit from the surplus produced by the *laboratores*, are best understood as lords rather than being solely comprised of nobles. It must be acknowledged that even this approach incurs its own problems. After all, not every fighter was necessarily a lord in the period and, while the great religious institutions acted as lords, most ecclesiasts were far from performing this role themselves. Still, this approach moves us further in the right direction and helps illustrate that, even in the period, ecclesiastical scholars made use of overlapping approaches to understand hierarchy.

Returning to the literary giant that is Wulfstan, we encounter once again the topic of the Three Orders in a letter sent to him by Ælfric. This letter, and perhaps even Ælfric's letter to Sigeweard, appear to have left a lasting impression on Wulfstan, for he later made use of the model in his own meditations on the correct ordering of a Christian society.[108] Surviving in a series of successive drafts, now known as the *Institutes of Polity*, these meditations consider the responsibilities of various sections of society, including the king, counsellors, bishops, nobles, reeves, priests, abbots, monks, nuns, laymen, widows, the Church, and even God.[109] In a section titled *Be cynestole* (*Concerning the Throne*), Wulfstan makes use of the Three Orders model and redeploys Ælfric's metaphor of three supports on which the throne stands:

> Ælc riht cynestol stent on þrim stapelum, þe fullice ariht stent: An is Oratores, and oðer is Laboratores, and þridde is Bellatores. Oratores syndon gebedmen, þe Gode sculon þeowian and dæges and nihtes for ealne þeodscipe þingian georne. Laboratores sindon weorcmen, þe tilian sculon, þæs þe eal þeodscipe big sceal libban. Bellatores syndon wigmen, þe eard sculon werian wiglice mid [w]æpnum. On þisum þrim stapelum sceal ælc cynestol standan mid rihte on cristenre þeode.

> Every just throne that stands fully as it should stands on three pillars: first, those who pray; second, those who labour; and third, those who fight. Those who pray are the clergy, who must serve God and fervently plead for all the people day and night. Those who labour are the workers who must toil for that by which the entire community may live. Those who fight are the warriors who must protect the land by waging war with weapons. On these three pillars must each throne rightly stand in a Christian polity.

---

[108] Moilanen, 'Society and Social Mobility', 1345–1346.

[109] This list is more or less in the order presented by Wulfstan. However, here, God is placed last rather than first. See Rabin, *The Political Writings of Archbishop Wulfstan of York*, 101–124.

Wulfstan changes the supports of the throne from *stela* (legs) to *stapol* (pillars) and, instead of Ælfric's emphasis upon the broken nature of the society surrounding him and the need for a remedy, he frames the structure as one which needs maintenance but remains strong. Wulfstan's rendition of the Three Orders model depicts each order like so: the *bellatores* are *wigmen* (war-men) who must defend the kingdom in a *wiglice* (warlike) manner; the *oratores* are *gebedmenn* (prayer-men) who *þingian* (plead) with God; and the *laboratores* are *weorcmen* (workmen) who *tilian* (toil) to ensure that everybody may live. Wulfstan's version of the model thus returns to the ambiguity of its earliest iteration in Alfred's translation of Boethius. There is no clear indication from which ranks these warriors and workers are drawn. Quite unlike the version penned by Ælfric and Wulfstan's own explicit treatment of rank in the *Geþyncðu* corpus, this represents quite a departure. Here, rank plays a minimal role and, instead, the function of each group in society is what is of paramount importance. For the purposes of stressing the economic unity of society and the need for harmony, Wulfstan chose to downplay rank-based forms of differentiation and, in its place, focus upon a different way of presenting the structures of society, one that stressed function.

3.4 *Maga, Unmaga*, and the Early English Legal Realm

Another way in which Wulfstan chose to conceptualise hierarchical relations in the period is expressed through the Old English words *maga* and *unmaga*. These words survive in the pre-Conquest literature of Alfred, Ælfric, and, most importantly for our purposes, Wulfstan. Yet to receive sustained scholarly attention, the word *unmaga* refers to someone who is either without means or helpless, such as a child or someone who is ill.[110] King Alfred's late ninth-century law code thus declares that: 'Gif hwa oðrum his unmagan oðfæste, 7 he hine on ðære fæstinge forferie, getriowe hine facnes se ðe hine fede, gif hine hwa hwelces teo' (If anyone entrusts a helpless (*unmagan*) individual to another, and they (the new guardian) cause or permit the death of those entrusted, they who previously supported the entrusted shall clear themself of suspicion, if anyone brings an accusation against them.)[111] Alfred's law indicates that the individual – the *unmaga* – in question is either a child or someone faced with serious physical or mental challenges. The former is strongly suggested in Ælfric's Old English translation of the story of Esther: ' ... 7 hæfde hi for dohtor, forðan þe hire dead wæs ge fæder ge modor, þa þa

---

[110] Bosworth, *An Anglo-Saxon Dictionary*, 1121.

[111] Af. §17; Jurasinski and Oliver, *The Laws of Alfred*, 311. This is quite a 'free' translation of the Old English which departs from the source's phrasing in favour of translating the sense of the passage. The meaning of the text and the contingent series of clauses is, hopefully, made clearer.

heo unmagu wæs' (. . . and he [Mordechai] took for a daughter [Esther], since she was an orphan/helpless, for her father and mother were dead).[112] When used in such contexts, *unmaga* did not connote subjugation or subordination, but rather a state of being unable to care for oneself due to minority or disability.

As an expression of relative political capability, however, *unmaga* can be found in the late tenth- and early eleventh-century laws of Æthelred and Cnut. As with many of their respective law codes, those in question appear to have been produced under the oversight of Wulfstan.[113] These texts portray a particular understanding of the differential in power between those of higher and lower rank and how such difference should be taken into consideration in the process of legal judgment:

> 7 swa man bið mihtigra her nu for worulde oþþan þurh geþingða hearra on hade, swa sceal he deoppor synna gebetan 7 ælce misdæda deoror agyldan, for þam þe se maga 7 se unmaga ne beoð na gelice, ne ne magon na gelice byrþene ahebban, ne se unhala þe ma þam halum gelice; 7 þy medmian 7 gescadlice toscadan, ge on godcundan scriftan ge on woroldcundan steoran, ylde 7 geogoþe, welan 7 wædle, hæle 7 unhæle, 7 hada gehwilcne. 7 gif hit geweorþeð, þæt man unwilles oþþe ungewealdnes ænig þing misdeð, na bið þæt na gelic þam þe willes 7 gewealdes sylfwilles misdeð; 7 eac se þe nydwyrhta bið þæs þe misdeð, se bið gebeorhges 7 þy beteran domes symle wyrðe, þe he nydwyrhta wæs þæs þe he worhte . . . 7 miltsige man for Godes ege 7 liþige man georne 7 beorge be dæle þam, þe þæs þearf sy.[114]

> Always, the more powerful a man here in the world, or the higher in privilege of rank, the more deeply should he amend his sins and the more dearly pay for every misdeed; *for the strong and the weak are not alike nor can they bear a like burden, any more than the sick are like the healthy.* Thus, one should moderate and distinguish reasonably, whether in religious penances or worldly punishments, between age and youth, wealth and poverty, health and sickness, and every category. And if it happen that anyone commits any misdeed involuntarily or unintentionally, that is not the same as he who offends of his own free will; so also he who does wrong under compulsion is always worthy of protection and of better judgment . . . And for fear of God, one should eagerly show mercy and leniency, and give such assurance (*beorge*) as there is need of.[115]

---

[112] Translation mine. Assman, ed., *Angelsächsische Homilien*, 94.
[113] Hudson, *Laws of England*, 90.   [114] Liebermann, *Die Gesetze der Angelsachsen*, 258.
[115] VI Atr 52–53, II Cn 68–68,3. Translation from Wormald, *Papers Preparatory*, 94. Italics my own, for emphasis. It is possible that this meditation on responsibility and accountability was motivated in part by the issue of corruption which seemed to trouble the Æthelredian regime and a lack of accountability among royal officials. See Upchurch, 'A Big Dog Barks'; Clayton, '*De Duodecim Abusiuis*', 156–163. Such an issue still seems to have troubled Wulfstan in one of his later sermons (Rabin, *The Political Writings of Archbishop Wulfstan of York,* 143–153).

This is a call to those who would fulfil the role of legal judge, that they might exercise restraint in deference to the relative social power of those involved in a case such as the *maga* and *unmaga*. If those in positions of higher influence were to perform illegal acts (or, more precisely in this context, sinful acts), they would be expected to pay a greater price to make amends. The inequality which ran throughout early medieval English society meant that, in practice, petitioners from lower ranks found the cards stacked against them in a court of law. Thus legal practice dictated that a higher-ranking individual was worth more to a defendant, for their word was given more weight as a compurgator (oath-helper).[116] Still, legal judgments in early medieval England often featured a healthy dose of compromise. In the laws of Æthelred, we find traces of the systemic preference for cases resolved by compromise (or 'love'): 'where a thegn has two choices, love (*lufe*) or law (*lage*), and he chooses love, that is to remain as binding as a judgment (*dom*)'.[117] Any agreement which reduced the need for the involvement and imposition of 'state' apparatus was attractive to the king and his representatives. As Andrew Rabin has observed, the 'priority was not to determine which claimant had the best legal case, but rather to find a compromise that would preserve the peace of the community'.[118] Although the leverage of relative social position most likely played a significant, if untraceable role in deciding the course of these early medieval equivalents of out-of-court settlements, there is a possibility that Wulfstan's exhortation for proportionate judgment was centred upon a pragmatic understanding that many cases were amorphous affairs which used the laws of the land as a guide rather than a strict rule.[119]

The pairing that Wulfstan favours, *se maga 7 se unmaga* (the strong and the weak), is, in the context of judicial pragmatism, used to stress the dissimilarity of the powerful and the powerless, with the intent to emphasise that each must be accountable in proportion to their situation. A more precise rendering of *maga* and *unmaga* acknowledges that these terms characterise an individual's strength or weakness in relation to their social or political power, or lack thereof.[120] So different are the politically strong and the politically weak from each other that it is comparable to the difference between one who is healthy (*hal*) and one is sick (*unhal*). It appears that, at least in this context, Wulfstan is linking the politically strong with the healthy and the politically weak with the

---

[116] Rabin, *Crime and Punishment*, 35–36, 49–50.

[117] III Atr. 13,3. Translation from Hudson, *Laws of England*, 90.

[118] Rabin, *Crime and Punishment*, 23.

[119] On use of law codes, see Cubitt, '"As the Lawbook Teaches"'; Roach, 'Law Codes and Legal Norms'.

[120] Bosworth, *An Anglo-Saxon Dictionary*, 664.

sick. While Wulfstan sees the less powerful as dependent in this legal context, just as one might see a sick patient as dependent upon or vulnerable to their healthy caregivers, his linguistic choices seem to stress the need for ethical social practice and care. The ordering of the qualities listed by Wulfstan respectively links political and social strength (*maga*) with wealth (*wela*), maturity (*ylde*), and health (*hal*), while political and social weakness (*unmaga*) is associated with poverty (*wædl*), youth (*geoguþ*), and sickness (*unhal*). There is certainly no reason to entertain that the youth of this list are envisaged as lacking vitality or occupying a position of vulnerability in the same sense as the ill. Though *ylde* can refer to old age, given that it often refers to senior members of a community, in this context it most likely refers to maturity, seniority, and, thus, influence within a community. Likewise, *geoguþ* indicates the state of being young or, simply, youth, which arguably implies immaturity, juniority, and, thus, less established ties within a community.[121] That the politically weak lack wisdom is, perhaps, a viable interpretation.[122] In short, the *unmaga* were understood to be unwise.

At the centre of Wulfstan's list of attributes is, nonetheless, a simple awareness that those with less power are vulnerable to predation from those who wield more, with power being measured in terms with which we may be more familiar: wealth, political influence, and social status. That those who are sick, poor, and young are vulnerable to mistreatment from those who are healthy, wealthy, and older is the message that unites these elements. Such an interpretation is reinforced by Wulfstan's concerns that those bound to a superordinate were vulnerable to coercion: 'if . . . anyone commits any misdeed involuntarily or unintentionally, that is not the same as he who offends of his own free will; so also he who does wrong under compulsion is always worthy of protection and of better judgment.'[123] It is the coercive dimensions of the 'vertical' power differential within a legal context that is the focus of Wulfstan's addition to the law codes of Æthelred and Cnut. Wulfstan's desire for proportionate judgments and an awareness that each defendant found guilty should bear a punishment proportional to their rank is borne from a pragmatic assessment of the inequity at work in early English society. A judge, in Wulfstan's eyes, was someone who could distinguish between the forces at play in a complex legal case and accommodate the needs of those who were most vulnerable.

---

[121] Bosworth, *An Anglo-Saxon Dictionary*, 384, 587.

[122] In support of such a reading, post-Carolingian riddles – written between the ninth and eleventh centuries – traced the heritage of the unfree rural inhabitants of France to Ham, the sinful and unwise third son of Noah. Likewise, Honorius Augustudunensis, who spent time in late eleventh- and early twelfth-century England, linked the fate of agricultural tenants and slaves to the impropriety of Ham (Freedman, *Images*, 99).

[123] VI Atr. 52, 2.

Wulfstan's use of the words *maga* and *unmaga* reveals a reading of power within early medieval England which may be considered alternative or supplemental to the Three Orders model. It evokes the continental framing of *pauper* (poor) and *potens* (powerful), a stark rendering of the exploitation of the poor by the powerful.[124] One could, perhaps, infer that these *unmaga* individuals are ceorls, people who could not represent and protect themselves without their lord's efforts or, indeed, from their lord. Yet it is telling that Wulfstan does not expressly link the ranks of ceorl and thegn to the weak and the powerful. Wulfstan makes it quite evident that a judge must be able to distinguish carefully between the various duties and responsibilities exercised by those with and without power and to apply the law respectively. Moreover, he exhorts that ecclesiasts must work to uphold what was just and be alert to the possibility of coercion. Therefore, the dependency depicted by the word *unmaga* is not one strongly linked to the labouring ranks specifically, but rather serves to denote a particular formation of vertical relations. This is, perhaps, the reason we do not find sources discussing a *hlaford* (lord) and his *unmagan* (weak men), but rather a *hlaford* and his *mannum* (men), *ceorlas* (peasants), or *þeowas* (slaves). Wulfstan sought to describe a problem which could develop within vertical relations, particularly as it pertained to the application of the law. It should, therefore, be no surprise that *unmaga* is never used as a label to categorise ceorls within law codes. Wulfstan saw that in order to best describe the issues which manifested within the legal realm, the terms *ceorl* and *thegn* would not serve him effectively. Rather, he needed to turn to the rarely used terms *maga* and *unmaga* to best capture a feature of vertical power relations.

3.5 *Rectitudines singularum personarum*

Rectitudines singularum personarum (hereafter *Rectitudines*), a treatise describing the obligations and duties of the inhabitants of an estate, provides a snapshot of the 'ideal' ordering of the late tenth- or early eleventh-century agrarian manor.[125] Beginning the document is a description of the role of the thegn on an estate:

> ÐEGEN LAGV IS þæt he sy his *boc rihtes* wyrðe . 7 þæt he ðreo ðinc of his lande do *fyrdfæreld* . 7 *burhbote* 7 *brycgeweorc* . eac of manegum landum mare landriht arist to cyniges gebanne swilce is. deorhege to cyniges hame 7

[124] Koziol, *The Peace of God*.

[125] *Rectitudines singularum personarum* (*Rectitudines*, cited as *RSP* followed by clause below) survives only in a twelfth-century copy (CCCC MS 383), but it is generally accepted that it was composed in the late tenth or early eleventh century. See Harvey, 'Rectitudines Singularum Personarum and Gerefa', 19.

scorp to friðscipe . 7 sæweard 7 heafodweard 7 fyrdweard . ælmesfeoh 7
cyricsceat 7 mænige oðere mistlice ðinge.

The law of the thegn is that he should be worthy of his *book-rights*, and that
from his land he [must] do three things: *levy a company, and be liable for the
building and repair of town walls, and build bridges*. Also, on many estates
more land-right is originated at the king's command such as [to maintain] the
animal-hedge for the king's estate, and [to supply] equipment for a defence
ship, and to guard the coast, and [to be a] head-guard and [to perform]
military watch, [to give] alms money and church tribute and many other
diverse things.[126]

The thegn will, it is assumed, invariably hold land and, so as to justify his
position, perform three services: provide military service, repair town walls, and
maintain bridges. Of particular importance, the text stipulates that these services
are not just to be performed to substantiate the thegn's rank but, more precisely,
validate their continued '*boc rihtes*', something often presumed to refer to the
ownership of bookland (land that was held by charter and was alienable, though
see Section 4 for issues with such a definition). One might see a certain
correspondence between this entry in *Rectitudines* and the image of thegnliness
sketched out in the *Geþyncðu* corpus. In those texts, it was the ability to control
five hides across several generations that acted as the marker of thegnly rank,
something which – in turn – was linked to clearly demarcated levels of compensation or wergild. Together, these texts produce a rather neat conceptual
package, with a well-ordered division between thegn and ceorl. This correspondence could be read as providing compelling evidence of the centrality of
bookland and five-hide estates in the construction of thegnly rank. However, the
shadowy hand of Wulfstan, which likely links both the *Rectitudines* and the
Geþyncðu texts, should give us reason to pause.

Rectitudines has long been mined for details regarding the administration and
relationships on pre-Conquest estates. Indeed, given how few sources we have
that depict the minutiae of the manor, it is very tempting to voraciously dissect
this account in pursuit of details. Yet its current form serves to offer a rendering
of the 'ideal' ordering of English society and the 'reciprocity' between inhabitants of the estate rather than being bound by the finer points of veracity. The
eminent Dorothy Bethurum, a specialist on Wulfstanian literature, identifies
several stylistic devices which, like a criminal's fingerprints at the scene of
a crime, indicate his presence in the construction of this text.[127] *Rectitudines* is
often taken to be a companion piece to *Gerefa*, a text that discusses the duties of

---

[126] Gobbitt, ed. and trans., *Gerefa*, 1. Hereafter, translation of *RSP* from Gobbitt. I have made a few,
very minor changes to Gobbitt's translation which I duly note. Italics my own, for emphasis.
[127] Bethurum, 'Six Anonymous Old English Codes'.

the reeve on an estate. Both pieces were likely not authored by Wulfstan in the first instance but were compiled and heavily edited by him at a later date. For this and other reasons, there are few who take the *Gerefa* as a practical instruction manual for running an estate, especially given the numerous and sizeable omissions within the text regarding key farming and administrative matters. Thus, as Paul Harvey notes, we should see '*Gerefa* as a literary exercise rather than as a didactic or administrative text'.[128] *Rectitudines* should be seen in a similar manner.[129]

While the *Rectitudines* in its earliest incarnations may have served as a more prosaic handbook of sorts to those who managed the ecclesiastical estates of St Peter's in Bath, the version which survives to us has been heavily curated by an ecclesiast invested in righting the social disorder left by Æthelred's reign.[130] The most telling sign of the text's reworking under Wulfstan and the broader purpose to which it was turned is the inclusion of a section on the thegn. Opening with the phrase 'ÐEGEN LAGV' (the law of the thegn), the first line of both this section and the entire document uses the only Scandinavian word in the text (a term which appears regularly elsewhere in Wulfstan's oeuvre).[131] All other sections make use of the Old English word '*riht*' to describe the obligations of each role. Moreover, the duties of the thegn, as described earlier in this Element, largely look outwards, beyond the confines of the estate and, consequently, the inclusion of this figure seems to run counter to the primary focus of the document. The social order depicted in this reworked version of *Rectitudines* is, therefore, one that no longer just details the finer workings of an estate, but rather stretches up into the upper echelons of society and details the obligations of a thegn to his king.

Below the rank of thegn, we are confronted with a plethora of specialised roles: *geneat* (tenant), *kotsetla* (cottager), *gebur* (peasant), *swane* (swineherd), *beoceorle* (beekeeper), *folgere* (follower (of the plough)), *sædere* (sower), *oxanhyrde* (oxherd), *cuhyrde* (cowherd), *sceaphyrdan* (shepherd), *gathyrde* (goatherd), *cyswyrhte* (cheese-wright), *berebrytte* (barley-keeper), *bydele* (beadle), *wudewarde* (wood-warden), the *hæigwerde* (hedge-warden), *mylewerde* (miller), *sutere* (shoemaker), and *leodgotan* (plumber).[132] The role of land suffuses this account and helps delineate between positions: the thegn has

---

[128] Harvey, 'Rectitudines Singularum Personarum and Gerefa', 9.
[129] Harvey is much more minded than I to accept that *Rectitudines* was 'systematic, comprehensive, and functional'. This may be a fair assessment of the putative original iteration, but Wulfstan extracted it from its context to provide an imprecise model to be applied more broadly. See Harvey, 'Rectitudines Singularum Personarum and Gerefa', 12.
[130] Harvey, 'Rectitudines Singularum Personarum and Gerefa', 20–21.
[131] Harvey, 'Rectitudines Singularum Personarum and Gerefa', 13.
[132] Gobbitt, ed. and trans., *Gerefa*, 1–29.1.

bookland, some pay rent (which appears to act as a marker of status), and others are allowed to occupy land solely through their labour. A useful survey referred to as the *Feudal Book*, which details the inhabitants of estates belonging to the Abbey of Bury St Edmunds, Suffolk, in the late 1080s, provides a useful point of comparison. In the lists surveying the hundreds of Blackbourn, Cosford, and Thedwestry, we find a treasure trove of occupational bynames, in (a) Latin: *aurifaber* (goldsmith), *bercarius* (shepherd), *clericus* (cleric), *diaconus* (deacon), *equarius* (groom), *faber* (smith), *hægweard* (hayward), *mango* (monger), *mercator* (merchant), *molendinarius* (miller), *pelliciarius* (perlterer), *pistor* (baker), *porcarius* (swineherd), *prepositus* (reeve), *presbiter* (priest), *sutor* (shoemaker), *textor* (weaver), and (b) Old English: *blodlætere* (blood-letter), *croppere* (tree-pruner), *dæge* (dairymaid), *heallemann* (hall-man), *horsthegn* (horse thegn), *hweolwyrhta* (wheelwright), *inngerefa* (inn-reeve), and *teper* (tapper/beer-seller).[133] In this way, we find some consistencies across both sources in the types of roles listed, such as shepherds, shoemakers, swineherds, and foresters.

Where differences emerge is that the survey from Bury St Edmunds provides a precise indication of how much land each tenant 'teneo' (holds) and how much they 'reddo' (render) to the institution: Uluric the shepherd held twenty acres and paid twenty denarii; Ulfuine the shoemaker held six acres and paid five denarii; Æluric the swineherd held one acre and paid one denarius; and Lemer the tree-pruner held three acres and paid one denarius and one obulum.[134] By comparison, *Rectitudines* provides a rather general sense of how much land such individuals may have held, stating that a gebur was to be given seven acres to settle the land and that a ploughman would earn two acres across the year.[135] What is particularly striking is that there is a large variety across these values, and that certain professions, such as shepherding, had the potential to hold more land than other occupations. For example, the *Feudal Book* records that Godman the smith held only one acre, as did both the mongers Eduine and Goduuine; Goduine the miller shared five acres with Ælric and Uluric; Ælfuine the goldsmith held seven acres; and Ælfstan the baker possessed ten acres.[136] Perhaps most surprising is that Godric the reeve held only three acres and Uluric the merchant held only seven acres.[137] Wulfstan's *Rectitudines* depicts a series of serried ranks, each of whom has explicit obligations to his superordinate and can expect certain things in return. More prosaic accounts from later in the

---

[133] Probert, 'Peasant Personal Names and Bynames'.
[134] MS Mm. iv.19, ff. 139b, 137, 135, 136b. See also Douglas, *Feudal Documents*, 35, 29, 25, 28.
[135] *RSP*, 4.2, 11.
[136] MS Mm. iv.19, ff 137b, 139, 137b, & 138(2)b; Douglas, *Feudal Documents*, 29, 37, 35, 30, 34.
[137] MS Mm. iv.19, ff. 142 & 136; Douglas, *Feudal Documents*, 40, 27.

eleventh century, such as the *Feudal Book*, seem to suggest that no such simple division existed.[138] Thus, less ideologically driven descriptions of the local social landscape of the manorial estate show a highly complex web of relationships.

The breadth of ambition which underpins Wulfstan's revisions to the text – to describe the fundamental ordering of estates and their overall place in the social hierarchy – contrasts starkly with the author's arguably myopic vision of the local landscape. The use of the word *æhtemann*, found almost exclusively in ecclesiastical sources, seems to suggest that the types of estates described in *Rectitudines* were those run by ecclesiastical institutions or, at least, that these were the types of estates with which the author was most familiar.[139] Indeed, the text has been linked to the Tidenham charter, which surveyed an estate belonging to Bath, and which features some similar phrases.[140] As an author who did not let the finer points of accuracy get in the way of making an important moral point, it would be entirely befitting Wulfstan's known rhetorical techniques that he repurposed the text of *Rectitudines* (and *Gerefa*) to suit his needs. The addition of a caveat that notes that these duties and obligations differed from estate to estate would seem a rather belated acknowledgement that these details were not entirely representative.[141] In short, Wulfstan's extension of his moral ideas into his attempts to detail the workings of local estates was, as Rosamond Faith articulates, a bid to exemplify the '"holiness of society": the structure of society was not simply a matter of social function but of moral order'.[142]

A section in *Gerefa* reveals the importance of maintaining a just and ordered existence on the estate:

> Symle he sceal his hyrmen scyr pan mid manunge to hlafordes neode 7 him eac leanian be ðam ðe hy earnian.
> Ne læte he næfre his hyrmen hyne oferwealdan ac wille he ælcne mid hlafordes creafte 7 mid folcrihte.
> Selre him his æfre of folgoðe ðonne on gyf hine magan wyldan ða ðe he scolde wealdan.
> Ne bið hit hlaforde ræd þæt he þæt ðafige.[143]

---

[138] A tenth-century charter documenting the transfer of ten holdings at Stoke-by-Hysseburne to the Old Minster at Winchester shows a different approach to recording the local hierarchy, recording only 'þa gerihta þæ ða ceorlas sculan don' (the rights and obligations which ceorls must do). There is no attempt to distinguish between tenants and tenurial differences. See S 359. See also Robertson, *Anglo-Saxon Charters*, 206–207.

[139] Lemanski, 'Æhtemann', 77–78. See also Faith, *The Moral Economy of the Countryside*, 54.

[140] On Tidenham see Faith, 'Tidenham, Gloucestershire, and the History of the Manor in England'.

[141] Harvey, 'Rectitudines Singularum Personarum and Gerefa', 19–20.

[142] Faith, *The Moral Economy of the Countryside*, 102. Lemanski, 'Æhtemann', 56–57. See also Harvey, 'Rectitudines Singularum Personarum and Gerefa', 20–22.

[143] Liebermann, *Die Gesetze der Angelsachsen*, 454; Gobbitt, ed. and trans., *Gerefa*, 6–7.

Similarly, he (the reeve) must inspire his subordinates with admonishments to the lord's need, and reward each of them as they merit.
He should never let his subordinate wield power over him, but he should direct each with the lord's power and with folkright.
(It is) better (use of) him (the reeve) if he is always out labouring than in (his position), if those whom he should govern would rule him.
It will not be the wise lord that endures this.[144]

In this account, it is needful that a reeve *manung* (admonish) labourers to do their duty, and they are to employ both rewards and punishments as circumstances dictated. The phrase 'he sceal his hyrmen scyr þan mid manunge' is more precisely translated as 'he (the reeve) must sharpen his subordinates with admonishment'. While acting as a metaphor for the act of inspiring labourers, the image of a reeve honing labourers as his tools is unmistakeable.[145] It may not be a coincidence that Alfred the Great likened the three orders to a king's 'tol' (tools).[146] Regardless, it is particularly telling that that the 'hlafordes neode' (lord's need) was the ultimate arbiter of what was necessary, and that the expectation of obedience permeates the text. There is an evident concern that the inhabitants of the estate might refuse to yield to the commands of the reeve. To resolve this, the reeve must invoke the lord's *cræft* – in this case meaning power, and further evoking a metaphor of trade or skill in the management of *hyrmen* – and *folcriht*, or folkright. The threat of a lord's power was, presumably, not always enough to ensure compliance among the labourers and calls to common custom remained a needed device of persuasion. This sense of justice and duty are emblematic of the ethical code that Wulfstan tried to convey throughout his works. Unlike the simpler ternary model or the binary models discussed earlier in this Element, this account offered a more detailed understanding of local society, one centred upon the language of reciprocal service and rewards. Still, it intersects quite neatly with his use of the binary and ternary models. Echoing the ternary model, all members of the estate must fulfil their function in order to keep the enterprise moving forward. The lord – the *maga* – must not abuse his power over the *unmaga* of his estate, but rather reward them fairly for their labour. It perhaps sits less comfortably alongside the *Geþyncðu* corpus, but there is a similar sense of order. Advancement can only come if an individual uses the correct routes, and the ownership of land remains a key quality of thegnliness. In this way, *Rectitudines* offers a fourth compelling model of early English society but one that is suffused with ideologically shaped abstractions.

---

[144] Gobbitt, ed. and trans., *Gerefa*, 22.8–22.11. For *hyrmen*, I have provided 'subordinates' where Gobbit translates as 'underlings'.
[145] Gobbitt, ed. and trans., *Gerefa*, 6. [146] Powell, 'The "Three-Orders"', 103–104.

For an individual who sought to draw clear demarcations between ceorls and thegns in his *Geþyncðu* treatise, it is telling that Wulfstan deployed different models according to the needs of his work. Sometimes the binary of ceorl and thegn sufficed. Elsewhere, he needed to stress the tripartite relationship between the *gebedmen* (prayer-men), *wigmen* (war-men), and *weorcmen* (workmen). When discussing improper judicial practice, he turned to binaries like *maga* and *unmaga*. Locating the moral order in the local landscape of estate management required a picture of many serried ranks, all of whom knew their place and received just rewards. In short, the end shaped the means. When it comes to our attempts to conceptualise status in the period, we could do worse than take inspiration from this pre-eminent social commentator of early medieval England, wielding an array of terms and deploying them as appropriate to the ends we seek.

4 The View from the 'Local'

4.1 Introduction

Having examined the proclamations of kings concerning their thegns and the meditations of an archbishop bound up in the world of court politics, I wish now to turn to evidence rooted in the localities of England. That is not, of course, to say that we will be looking at experiences of hierarchy through the eyes of locals – invariably, non-nobles remain the objects of documentation rather than the subject producing such descriptions. Still, this section focuses upon granular forms of documentation which allow for a more nuanced window into the day-to-day 'realities' of how the hierarchy of early medieval England functioned. Given the need for brevity, this section concentrates upon three types of sources – charters, manumissions, and guild records – and, wherever possible, supplements the findings with archaeological data (including excavations of manor-house sites and zooarchaeological finds).

To speak of charters is to refer to a remarkably broad category, which includes everything from diplomas issued by kings to the wills of ecclesiasts and laypeople. For the purposes of this section, the charters selected provide us a window into the important roles that subordinates could play in dispute settlement and permit the consideration that leased land, or loanland, may have served in the construction of social status and the acquisition of higher rank. Building upon this initial picture of the inconsistent relationship between power, rank, and tenurial status, an examination of manumissions and status-documents reveals that the lower strata of society in South West England were busily gaining influence throughout the tenth and eleventh centuries. Ecclesiastical institutions at Bodmin, Cornwall, and Exeter, Devon, began to record the names of witnesses who lay beyond the nobility, allowing for the inference that networks of local notables were beginning to emerge. Usually undetected as active participants in legal proceedings elsewhere in the corpus of material from early medieval England, these manumissions show non-nobles as influential actors on the stage of local politics. Rounding out the section, an interrogation of guild statutes shows these to be ideal venues for the intense types of social jockeying discussed by Robin Fleming and Christine Senecal. As seen in the statutes of the Thegns' Guild from Cambridgeshire, these associations could present opportunities for those threatened by social climbing to enact forms of social closure; they often also seem to have invited intense forms of networking, evidenced in the guild lists from the hinterlands of Exeter.

Altogether these sources show a much more complicated and messier picture than is revealed in the many of the oft-consulted source types. The blurred boundaries postulated by Senecal are thus better documented. More than this, these case-studies allow us to identify both moments and vectors by which inconsistencies across the values of rank and power could emerge. In short, this section illustrates that an individual's overall status in early English society was constructed via a variety of factors, and it was through the spaces discussed in what follows that the potential meaning(s) and value(s) of social signifiers, such as the rank of thegn, were renegotiated, reshaped, and redeployed across the course of the tenth and eleventh centuries.

4.2 Charters

The lower strata of society are poorly represented in surviving legal material, especially those documents which record active engagement within legal processes. Early English charters documented the conveyance of property, usually bookland, from one party to another, which rarely involved people beyond spheres of thegnhood and nobility. Rather than standing solely on their own merit, these documents worked in tandem with an oral agreement reached in front of a wider meeting, perhaps in front of an assembly at the royal, shire, or local hundred court (shire and hundreds being territorial units of administration).[147] The majority of surviving charters record important named witnesses who were willing to testify to the terms of the deal. In almost all instances, those considered to be suitable named witnesses were

---

[147] See Insley, 'Assemblies and Charters'.

bishops, ealdormen, ecclesiasts, king's thegns, and thegns.[148] Even noble-men were sometimes referenced via collective descriptions. In a fierce land dispute between a mother and son in early eleventh-century Herefordshire, it is recorded that she bid that 'eallum þam godan mannum' (all the good men) attending the *moot*, or meeting, would bear witness to her decision not to leave anything to her son. In some instances, who comprised the 'good men' witnessing certain transactions may have extended beyond the thegnhood, but in many cases, it seems clear that it was intended to denote only the upper echelons of society. Lower-ranking individuals may be glimpsed in the record as part of the several hundreds who were in attendance along with 'all the leading men', but this is largely the extent of their visible activities in charters.[149] This should be of no surprise when being of higher rank meant that your word was worth more in a court of law.[150] Patrick Wormald argued that judicial appeal was made not to written law in the main, but to 'collective judgement in an atmosphere of public witness', a group to which 'local standing was the major qualification for membership'.[151] Such power formed an imposing force which made the law courts a largely forbidding and inaccessible location for the peasant. It was this phenomenon, as dis-cussed in Section 3, which vexed Wulfstan so greatly. The social and polit-ical power of the *maga* over the *unmaga* was never so starkly realised as in the domain of law.

It must be noted, however, that power did not necessarily flow in one direction and those who lay outside of the thegnhood or nobility could exert a profound influence on some legal proceedings. In a late eleventh-century legal dispute between Bishop Wulfstan II of Worcester (*c.*1008–1095) and Abbot Walter of Evesham (r. 1077/8–d. 1104) – which centred upon rights over sake-and-soke, burial dues, church-scot, customs, and military service across the estates of Hampton and Bengeworth in Oswaldslow, Worcester – a steersman named Eadric played a decisive role in deciding the outcome.[152] Both plaintiff and defendant came prepared to plead for their cause on the agreed day. Wulfstan put his faith in a cadre of 'legitimos testes … qui tempore regis Edwardi hoc viderant' (law-worthy witnesses … who knew the situation before 1066), while Walter preferred to mobilise the corpse of St Egwin to bolster his

---

[148] A king's thegn held land directly from the king. Common thegns held land from other members of the nobility.

[149] Keynes and Kennedy, *The Libellus Æthelwoldi Episcopi*, § ii.11, ii.11a, ii.25 & ii.48, 6, 7, 10, 16, 23.

[150] Rabin, *Crime and Punishment*, 49–50.   [151] Wormald, 'Conclusion', 215–219.

[152] Bishop Wulfstan of Worcester on this occasion is not to be confused with his predecessor of the same name, Archbishop Wulfstan of York, who wrote key pre-Conquest texts discussed elsewhere in this Element.

claim.[153] Evidently, the presence of St Egwin's body did not prove enough to sway those assembled nor the judges. Rather, it was Wulfstan's witnesses who would take the day and secure his rights in the region. The importance of witnesses who knew how things had been before the Norman Conquest of 1066 offers a slim but useful window into earlier legal practice.

Wulfstan's key witness was Eadric, 'qui fuit tempore regis Edwardi sterman-nus navis episcopi, et ductor exercitus eiusdem ad servitium regis' (who had been the steersman of the bishop's ship in King Edward's day and who had led the bishop's army on the king's service) but, at the time of the court hearing, held land from Bishop Robert of Hereford (d. 1095), also known as Robert the Lotharingian. During a *probatio* (examination) of the evidence, Eadric's impartiality appears to have been stressed: 'et hic erat homo Rodberti Herefordensis episcopi, ea die qua sacramentum optulit et nichil de episcopo W(lstano) tenebat' (he was the man of Bishop Robert of Hereford, and on the day that the oath was taken, held nothing of Bishop Wulfstan).[154] This legal dispute, therefore, likely began after 1078, as Walter of Evesham took office in 1077/8, and, after several meetings, was completely resolved by 1086, as indicated in the records of the *Greater Domesday Book*.[155] Though Eadric cannot be located in records from 1086 onwards, there was an individual of this name listed in the *Greater Domesday Book*, who held a five-hide estate worth only one-and-a-half pounds in Hindlip and Offerton, near Worcester, in the time of King Edward.[156] This identification seems even more certain given that the tenant-in-chief of this estate in 1086 was Bishop Wulfstan and the final settlement of this long-running dispute featured a witness called Edric of Hindlip.[157] Given the location of his holdings and that Eadric no longer held the estate in 1086 nor can be identified as holding any land afterwards, this case played out between these two dates. It may even have taken place as late as 1085, given that a charter from Hereford records that a certain Edricus de uuendloc (Eadric of Wenlock, Gloucestershire) acted as a witness to a payment of twenty solidi by Roger De Lacy to Bishop Robert for a lifetime lease of Holme Lacy on St Martin's Day of that year.[158] The legality of the manoeuvrings made by Wulfstan and Robert behind the scenes may be somewhat questionable; after all, they appear to have been close friends.[159] Regardless, Eadric was no longer the steersman of Wulfstan's ship

---

[153] Bates, *Regesta Regum Anglo-Normannorum*, 998. The translation follows that of Bates.

[154] Bates, *Regesta Regum Anglo-Normannorum*, 997–998.   [155] GDB WORC 2,1.

[156] GDB WORC 2,52.   [157] Wormald, 'Lordship and Justice', 322.

[158] There are actually two witnesses named Eadric, but the second is identified by his byname Dapifer, meaning someone who brings food to a table. See Galbraith, 'An Episcopal Land-Grant of 1085', 371–372.

[159] 'On the fourth day the body [of Wulfstan] was buried by Robert, Bishop of Hereford, long bound to him in holy friendship' (Winterbottom and Thomson, *Gesta pontificum Anglorum*,

nor holding what I suspect was leased land, given its reversion to his former lord, and thus became the lynchpin of his case against Walter.

So important was Eadric to the clinching of this fraught case that he was singled out above 'multi alii seniores et nobiles' (many other elderly and noble men), some of whom we know were either very wealthy or had held socially influential positions, such as the sheriff of Worcestershire.[160] Though Eadric seemingly held much less property than the other named witnesses, his testimony held particular weight in a system designed to promote the authority of those of higher rank. Those in higher positions of privilege required, from time to time, the support of those ranked much lower down the standard sociopolitical hierarchy. In this case, Eadric the steersman was a highly experienced individual in charge of a very expensive piece of technology, and the combination of his skill set and service afforded a certain degree of prestige. He managed to leverage his knowledge and labour into such a level of social cachet that he was more valuable to Wulfstan in the legal realm than his more wealthy associates. This may, of course, be an imperfect example for the purposes of this section, given the possibility that Eadric held, at least at one point, five hides and potentially could have ranked as a thegn. Still, even if he held the rank of thegn, it is telling that Eadric does not seem to have been afforded the non-institutional honorific in the documents which survive. His other accomplishments were more pertinent to the demonstration of his position in society. Moreover, what matters most is that he enjoyed significant prestige above and beyond what one might expect for someone of his social standing precisely because of the service he had rendered. A significant proportion of society pursued such a route, putting their skills to work in service to a lord who would offer them patronage and/or commendation.[161] This, in turn, may have led to the kind of social currency enjoyed by Eadric.

It is very easy to erect in our minds a clear division between ceorl and thegn, particularly one based on tenurial status. As discussed earlier, the work of Archbishop Wulfstan II of York is a tricky beast to handle and clauses 2 and 9 of *Geþyncðu* and *Norðleoda laga* respectively are perhaps the trickiest: both refer to five hides as a requisite amount needed for a ceorl to attain the wergild of a thegn. Ann Williams has argued that the stipulation in *Geþyncðu* – that a ceorl's *agenes lands* (own lands) had to be held *fullice* (fully) – indicates that they were required to be in possession of bookland (*bocland*) – that is, land often taken by scholars to have been held by charter and which could be freely

---

439). Wormald highlights some further attempts made by Wulfstan to manipulate the case (Wormald, 'Lordship and Justice', 321–322).

[160] Bates, *Regesta Regum*, 998.

[161] On commendation, see Baxter, 'Lordship and Justice'. On the need for an advocate, see Rabin, 'Old English *Forespeca*'.

alienated.[162] It is entirely possible that *fullice* serves in this context to indicate bookland, though I do find it curious that Wulfstan did not simply state that. Rather, I propose that an alternative reading would imply that *Norðleoda laga* does not necessarily corroborate Williams's claims on this matter. The word used in this text, *hæbban*, can simply mean 'to hold'. Rabin's translation, quoted earlier, deftly captures the ambiguity of *Norðleoda laga*, and what seems to have mattered most was not necessarily that one must have held bookland, but rather that one had the ability to hold land in such a way that the three services – the aforementioned *trinoda necessitas* – most associated with bookland could be discharged effectively.[163] If this were the case, it is possible that leased land might have served to exceed the five-hide threshold, assuming that it actually held any weight in day-to-day social practice. An example from the mid eleventh century, recorded in the *Liber Eliensis*, provides an account which may support that – although there was a legal and economic distinction – there was little social distinction between leased land and land held by charter. For example, Guthmund, brother of Abbot Wulfric of Ely, was allegedly forced to lease land from his brother because his offer of marriage had been rejected by the daughter of a powerful nobleman. According to this account, despite his noble status (he is described as *nobilis*), Guthmund did not hold the required 'lordship of forty hides of land', which would rank him among the upper echelons of society.[164] To make up this shortfall, he leased land from the abbey (though only with the knowledge of Wulfric, who kept the deal a secret and made no 'written witness'). Soon after, the marriage contract was agreed.[165] The would-be bride and her family may not have chosen to distinguish between the ways in which he held parts of his property portfolio – something that may have been characteristic of the different approaches to record-keeping and landholding in eastern England.[166] Or else, quite simply, Guthmund kept the truth of the matter hidden, just as his brother Wulfric kept the lease secret from his monks. One can imagine that discretion may have been a preferable option for many would-be lords living on leased land.

Certainly, the place of leased land in the property market may have been more mainstream than the relatively small number of surviving leases suggests. No small amount of work has been undertaken upon the corpus of 147 leases which survive from pre-Conquest England. Stephen Baxter and John Blair have concluded that royal *lænland* (loanland) – land granted to the king's men and

---

162 Williams, 'A Bell-House and a Burh-Geat', 27.
163 Many thanks must go to Alice Taylor for her helpful suggestions and feedback on this matter.
164 Williams, *The World before Domesday*, 4; Fairweather, *Liber Eliensis*, ii:97, 198.
165 Fairweather, *Liber Eliensis*, ii:97, 198–200.
166 Blair, 'The Limits of Bookland', 229–252.

then potentially reclaimed after the termination of service – was an important facet of the early 'aristocratic' experience.[167] These lords may not have paid rent in the same sense as manorial tenants on *gafolland*, but payment or service was provided to secure the right to temporarily inhabit the land. The acquisition of loanland may even have offered an alternative route to 'intensive lordship'.[168] Loanland could, perhaps, eventually be transformed into bookland. As much is suggested by King Alfred's version of St Augustine's *Soliloquies*, in which he describes a situation where loanland could turn into bookland:

> Ælcne man lyst, siððan he ænig cotlyf on his hlafordes læne myd his fultume gitimbred hæfð, þæt he hine mote hwilum þar-on gerestan ... and his on gehwilce wisan to þere lænan tilian, ægþær ge on se ge on lande, oð þone fyrst þe he bocland and æce yrfe þurh his hlafordes miltse geearnige.[169]

> Every man likes, when he has built up a farm on his lord's lease with his help, to stay there some time ... and to work for himself on the lease both on sea and on land, and till the time when he shall earn book land and eternal inheritance through his lord's kindness.[170]

Although this passage very much served as a metaphor for salvation, it may not be entirely removed from daily practice. A lease issued by Bishop Oswald of Worcester in the tenth century granted two and a half hides to 'cynelme his þegne to boc londe swa he hit him ær hæfde toforlætan to læn londe' (to his thegn Cynelm as bookland just as he had granted it before as loanland).[171] From the body of surviving leases, we find examples of *cneohtas* (sing. *cniht*, non-noble retainers) receiving loanland, perhaps acting as staging posts on the way to bookland.[172] Still, these examples from Worcester may be less clear-cut than previously thought. Blair has recently argued that these are not cases of loanland becoming transmuted into bookland, but rather that the booking process merely meant that the 'three-life' loan was recorded in 'some kind of document'.[173] The idea of bookland and perpetual inheritance were not necessarily as closely coupled as they have been traditionally taken to be by scholars. If this is the case, then the *bocland* of Wulfstan's *Geþyncðu* and *Norðleoda laga* may either have referred to land that was held by some variety of means (bookland,

---

[167] Keynes and Lapidge, ed. and trans., *Alfred the Great*, 139; Baxter and Blair, 'Land Tenure'; Keynes, 'Mercia and Wessex', 325–326. See also Wormald, '*On þa wæpnedhealfe*'.

[168] Pratt, 'Demesne Exemption', 27.   [169] Carnicelli, ed., *King Alfred's Version*, 48.

[170] Baxter and Blair, 'Land Tenure', 19. See also Smith, *Land and Book*, 122–135.

[171] S 1347. See Earle, *A Hand-Book to the Land*, 208.

[172] S 1326 & S 1332. See Robertson, *Anglo-Saxon Charters*, 97, 115. See also King, 'St. Oswald's Tenants', 100–113.

[173] Blair, 'The Limits of Bookland', 220–222.

loanland, or otherwise) and recorded by *boc* or described bookland in the traditional sense in an attempt to reset both blurred social and tenurial boundaries.

Some landholders did not always take the legal path towards trying to retain loanland. A certain Beahmund of Holland, who had held a marsh and fishery from St Æthelthryth's in Ely, Cambridgeshire, for more than fifteen years in return for a rent of two thousand eels, used this as a means to claim yet more land. After six years of failed suits, Bishop Æthewold eventually managed to reclaim all of this land, but evidently reclaiming loaned (and even un-loaned) land was no small feat.[174] In the case discussed previously, Guthmund refused to return the land following the marriage ceremony and even after Wulfric's death. Having no legal document to prove the land was leased, the abbey was forced to bargain. Guthmund used his possession of the land to reach an agreement that he might hold the land for the rest of his life.[175] This problem may well have been much more widespread. As Stephen Baxter has noted, Worcester struggled to reclaim some of its three-life leases during the tribulations faced by the Æthelredian regime, apparently resorting to reluctantly extending them for a fourth life.[176]

I suspect that loanland played a significant role in the thriving of ceorls and would-be thegns and potentially served to blur locals' sense of lords' relative property portfolios. It cannot be contested that the intimate knowledge of the land possessed by locals (termed *dense local knowledge* by Julio Escalona) was vital to producing stable boundaries between estates.[177] Similarly, the testimonies provided by juries of thegns after the Conquest of 1066 proved useful for the Domesday commissioners in creating their infamous record of tenurial holdings.[178] Still, one might wonder how accurate these accounts were in trying to establish how absent members of the community had previously held land, especially if Blair is correct in his assertion that there was 'a significant blurring of boundaries' between bookland and loanland.[179] Together, such uncertainties,

---

[174] Fairweather, *Liber Eliensis*, ii:24, 120–121.

[175] Fairweather, *Liber Eliensis*, ii:97, 199–200.

[176] Baxter, 'Archbishop Wulfstan and the Administration of God's Property', 176.

[177] Escalona, 'Dense Local Knowledge', 353. See also Escalona, 'Territorialidad e identidades'. As Alexander Langlands notes, this was remarkably effective and there is only one account of a dispute centred upon the actual boundaries of a plot of land and, tellingly, the associated charter listed no boundary clause. Still, Della Hooke reminds us that several place names refer to disputes and that these had long been areas of 'no man's land' (Langlands, 'Local Places', 389; Hooke, *Landscape*, 78–80). See also Lowe, 'Anglo-Saxon Boundary Clause', 63–100.

[178] Lewis, 'Domesday Jurors'. On the often-particular focus of the surveyors, see Thorn, 'Non Pascua sed Pastura'.

[179] Blair, 'The Limits of Bookland', 223. Further blurring such boundaries was thegnland, a type of 'precarious tenure' that pertained to 'typically smaller parcels of land'. See Williams, *The World before Domesday*, 81.

when taken alongside attempts of lessees to wrest their land from the hands of the lessors, likely produced a rather complex tenurial landscape that made judgments about precedence based on landholding patterns far less accurate in person than one may tempted to conclude from looking at such records today. Some of those in possession of a charter that ensured their unequivocal ownership over land likely advertised it far and wide, but it was not the only way to forge a claim, and others still may have chosen diverse routes to cement their place as a landowner in the local community.[180]

Even once an aspiring family had managed to secure bookland, it was not the sunlit fields of freedom one might assume. As David Pratt observes: 'The landholder's lifestyle would not be transformed by the gift of bookland, but rather secured with greater permanence.'[181] The gravity of gaining permanent control over land was undoubtedly significant, else it would not have been so sought after. Still, as long as the land and its appurtenances were returned in their original condition, an aspiring lord could manage his loaned land as intensely as he might. Indeed, we even find evidence of wealthy individuals giving up bookland for access to loanland, presumably because the latter would ultimately prove more profitable.[182] The path to greater wealth and greater rank was not always the straight line of an individual moving along the modernist, idealised trajectory from loanland to bookland. Moreover, bookland did not render one free from obligation and obedience. Whatever the finer points of the land market may have been, leasing land was likely a useful stepping stone for aspirants who wished to invest in potentially lucrative land and act in a lordly manner. This is perhaps why a charter of 984 records that King Æthelred gave to his thegn Brihtric eight hides that had formerly been held by Ætheric, 'quidam rusticus' (who was a peasant).[183] The concepts of bookland and thegn did not necessarily always align.

Thus, the kinds of concerns about social mobility that one can detect in the Wulfstanian corpus were likely exacerbated by the blurred distinctions between the various ways land might be 'held'. Alongside the potential confusion around tenurial precedence, archaeological evidence points to a heightened atmosphere of social competition in the tenth and eleventh centuries. Before the tenth century the archaeological remains of elite spaces are often hard to distinguish from other domestic environments. It may be that, in the earlier period, those with higher rank were not so driven as their later counterparts to separate themselves from others. As Blair has shown, lordly halls begin to make their mark on the landscape soon after the tenth century began in earnest. From 900

---

[180] Blair, 'The Limits of Bookland', 224–225.
[181] Pratt, 'Demesne Exemption', 27. See also Baxter and Blair, 'Land Tenure', 19–23.
[182] S 1420. See Robertson, *Anglo-Saxon Charters*, 143–145.   [183] S 855.

onwards, a new 'angle-sided form' of hall had become popular among what are presumed to be even lower-status thegnly circles. In the third quarter of the tenth century, evidence from the East Midlands suggests that a new preference for halls to be designed in the 'long-range' style became common. This fashionable form, with its many private chambers and an elevated room at one end, seems to have swept in from Flanders, an important trading partner. By the 980s, this trend had already lost force, to be replaced by a preference for 'traditional' aisled halls.[184] Alongside the remains of these buildings, textual evidence points to the importance that an elite was expected to maintain on his estate a *burhgeat* (enclosure-gate), *circan* (church), and *kycenan* (kitchen).[185] While we cannot in most cases match excavated estates to the manner in which they were held (i.e., as loanland or bookland), all of this seems to suggest that those with wealth were spending it lavishly to ensure their compounds reinforced social divisions as much as they might.

Architectural changes were, as Robin Fleming and Naomi Sykes have argued, matched by changes in consumption patterns. Osteoarchaeological evidence suggests that the rich and powerful came to dominate the consumption of and dictate access to various animals, including game animals and various seafoods.[186] Moreover, the year 1000 seems to have marked the intensification of chicken farming practices and the rise of commercial fishing, presumably with the intent to support a burgeoning demand for such wares among those who could afford them.[187] Contemporaneously, a wide range of forces, including marriage, deaths, and the acquisition of new offices, all served to increase land circulation among laymen, of whom some small proportion may well have been ambitious up-and-comers.[188] It is no coincidence that the resonances of the Old English word *rice* – a word which Malcolm Godden has shown had once overwhelmingly been used to denote power – began to take on the additional association of wealth around the first millennium.[189] All of this data, when taken together, indicates that the appearance of wealth and the performativity of the status had become ever more pressing. Presumably other social delineators, including tenurial status, were less effective than they previously had been.

---

[184] Blair, *Building*, 356–361.

[185] Liebermann, *Die Gesetze der Angelsachsen*, 456–469. See also Williams, 'A Bell-House and a Burh-Geat'.

[186] Sykes, 'Deer, Land, Knives and Halls'; Fleming, 'The New Wealth'.

[187] McClain and Sykes, 'New Archaeologies of the Norman Conquest', 95–96.

[188] Naismith, 'The Land Market and Anglo-Saxon Society', 29. 'The category of "Other layman", as opposed to "Thegns", "Thegn and partner", "Reeve" forms 21 percent of the buyers of Anglo-Saxon land and 26 percent of the sellers (second only to the king)' (Naismith, 'The Land Market and Anglo-Saxon Society', 22–23, 40). See also Campbell, 'The Sale of Land'.

[189] Godden, 'Money, Power and Morality'.

4.3 Manumissions

From the rural landscape surrounding Bodmin, Cornwall, and the hinterlands of Exeter, Devon, this potential for prosperity is manifested in a body of material unmatched elsewhere in England: manumissions. Approximately 120 survive from England, with the bulk originating from the south-west. A type of document that records when a slave is freed from their bondage, manumissions mark a profound moment of social transformation – one in which a slave moves 'up' through society to a less unfree rank. To be accurate, not all documents in this corpus are, in truth, manumissions, recording instead the sale and transfer of a slave from one owner to another. For this reason, the term *status document* has been preferred by some scholars.[190] The transition of slave to freeperson marked in the documents has drawn the attention of scholars such as Oliver Padel, David Pelteret, Duncan Probert, Frances Rose-Troup, and Alice Rio.[191] Nevertheless, all of these and other such studies primarily focus on the 'change of status' experienced by those manumitted. For the purposes of this section, however, it is the witnesses of these events on whom the focus now falls.

As with charters, manumissions listed the names of key figures who would be able and willing to attest that the act took place, thus ideally ensuring the enduring legitimacy of the ceremony. These ceremonies took place in a variety of locations, but usually in a highly visible venue that had some spiritual resonances. For instance, those manumissions enacted in Bodmin between *circa* 939 and *circa* 1075 took place either 'æt þere cirican dura æt Bodmine' (at the church door of Bodmin) or 'super altare sancti Petroci' (on the altar of St Petrock).[192] The manumissions which took place within Exeter and its hinterlands were enacted beyond the direct confines of ecclesiastical spaces, with some even being performed *on feower wegas* (at the four roads, i.e., crossroads).[193] As the tenth century waxed and waned, those freeing slaves and witnessing their elevation to free status began to include those beyond the clergy and nobility.

Early examples from Bodmin note a pool of witnesses comprised of priests, mass-priests, deacons, and unnamed collectives, referred to via suitably vague formulations – for example, 'idoneis testibus' (suitable witnesses), 'godera manna' (good men), or 'alii quam-plurimi de bonis hominibus' (some many other good people).[194] The witness lists of manumissions taking place after the turning of the

---

[190] For an excellent account of slavery in pre-Conquest England, see Pelteret, *Slavery in Early Medieval England*.

[191] Rose-Troup, 'Exeter Manumissions'; Pelteret, *Slavery in Early Medieval England*; Padel, *Slavery in Saxon* Cornwall; Probert, 'Exeter's Gildship and Manumission Records'; Rio, *Slavery after Rome*.

[192] The dating of these manumissions remains contested. For further discussion, see Pracy, 'Social Mobility', 9.

[193] Pelteret, *Slavery in Early Medieval England*, 134–138.

first millennium began to include a much larger pool of laymen, naming locally important characters. Witnessing the manumission of Ælfgyth, freed by a certain Æthelflæd, was a range of individuals, including priests, a thegn, a scribe, a reeve, a 'consul', and several men who were identified only by their forename and a byname. Many decades later, after the Norman conquest of England, this pattern of a broader range of witnesses continued. A man, named Maccos, both freed a woman named Codgiuo, and took the toll in two different manumissions. Described as a hundredman – someone who represented the administrative unit nominally comprising a hundred hides – this locally influential individual may not have held the rank of thegn. Indeed, Oliver Padel even speculated that Maccos was an imported slave who, having been freed, worked his way up the administrative system.[195] Whatever the case may be in this particular instance, scribes were not always taking the opportunity to stress a witness's thegnly rank and were choosing, or being instructed, to stress different attributes, such as official positions or functions or even distinctive attributes.

Turning to the manumissions which were enacted in Exeter, those witnessing such locally important legal processes included a *batsswegen* (boatswain), *faber* (craftsman), *webba* (weaver), and *coc* (cook).[196] A good example of the type of manumissions executed in Exeter is to be found in the transaction between Ælfgifu and Manegot, the former purchasing and freeing Hig, Dunna, and their children from the latter's control:

> Her kyð on þisse bec þ aeilgyuu gode (dat) alsyde hig 7 dunna 7 heora ofspring, aet mangode to .xiii. mancson, 7 aeignulf port gerefa, 7 Godric gupa namon þ toll, on manlefes ge wittnisse, 7 on leowerdes healta, 7 on leowines his broþor, 7 on aelfrices maphappes, 7 on sweignis scyldwirhrta, 7 haebbe he godes curs, þe þis aefre un do aon ecnysse. Amen.

> Here it is made known in this book that Aelfgifu 'the Good' freed Hig and Dunna and their progeny from Manegot for thirteen mancuses, and Einulf the port reeve and Godric 'Buttock' took the toll in the presence of Manleof and Leofweard 'the Lame' and Leofwines, his brother, and Aelfric, son of Happ, and Sweinn the shieldmaker. And may he have God's curse who may ever reverse this, always into eternity. Amen.[197]

The last-named witness to this exchange was Sweinn the *scyldwirhrta* (shield-maker). While the rank held by Einulf and Godric – who took the toll – or Manleof, Leofweard, and Ælfric – who witnessed alongside Sweinn is unclear,

[194] *Bodmin*, nos. 21, 30, 31.
[195] Padel, *Slavery in Saxon Cornwall*, 14–15; Insley, 'Kings and Lords', 21.
[196] Pracy, 'Social Mobility', 15–17.   [197] *Leofric Missal*, no. 253.4.

it seems likely that Sweinn, described by his trade, was not a member of the nobility. After all, a whole street in York – Skeldergate – was named for the numerous shield-makers who worked there. Compared to earlier examples, where almost all witnesses were drawn from the ecclesiastical community, the witness lists of manumissions had slowly become dominated by secular indi-'viduals, some of whom lay somewhere at the juncture between ceorls and minor thegns. That is not to say that the ecclesiastical world had abrogated its duties in recording these proceedings by the late eleventh century – if it had, we would not have such texts to consult today – but it was no longer the main force orchestrating these events. The impetus behind the creation of these status documents were people lower down the social spectrum, individuals who were developing the wealth to engage in such activity and accruing the social influence to warrant appearing in, or drawing together, an assembly of locally important social actors recorded in the witness lists.

At the intersection between a widening group of non-noble individuals who were able to free slaves and those witnessing such transactions sits a manumission in which 'liueger se bacestere on excestre alysde an wifman Ediþ hatte Godrices doht' cocraca ut of clist lande at Gosfreige bisceope to xxx p' (Leofgar (or Liveger) the Baker of Exeter released a certain woman called Eadgyth (or Edith), daughter of Godric 'Cock's-throat', out of Clyst-land from Bishop Geoffrey (of Coutances) for 30 pence).[198] Leofgar, a baker, was capable of accumulating enough capital to purchase and subsequently free someone held in bondage.[199] Such transactions were now drawing a crowd of witnesses, including those who may have sat beyond the traditional boundaries of nobility, such as Eadric 'se cipa' (the merchant).[200] Narrowing down the actual rank of a merchant remains a particularly challenging task, given that both thegns and ceorls appear to have operated as merchants, but this problem highlights the very plasticity of such social boundaries.[201] A subsequent account documents that a certain Hubert of Clyst sought to overturn the manumission of Eadgyth, highlighting that Leofgar freed her so that any children that they had or might have would have been born outside of bondage.

---

[198] Translation mine. Old English found in Chambers, Förster, and Flower, *The Exeter Book*, no. 25. See also Pracy, 'Social Mobility', 18.

[199] Elaine Treharne has argued that Eadgyth (or Edith as she prefers to translate the name) possessed a status that 'suggests she would be a freewoman' (it is unclear why this is the case) and thus this was not a manumission but rather represented the ceremonial admittance of an individual to a guild. Treharne's argument, though highly speculative, may have some merit to the broader corpus, but not all of the Exeter manumissions, such as the freeing of Eadgyth, seem to comfortably fit this explanation. Even should Treharne's argument be correct in part, it becomes rather hard to establish what is a manumission and what documents the admittance to a guild. That the majority of these records are manumissions or document the purchase of the unfree seems to remain the prevailing view. See Treharne, 'The Conners of Exeter', 21–25.

[200] Pracy, 'Social Mobility', 18.   [201] Fleming, 'Rural Elites and Urban Communities', 17–18.

This desire to free a loved one or oneself resulted in a situation whereby individuals managed to free themselves from bondage for significant sums, such as a certain Godwin the Black who paid fifteen shillings (three quarters of a pound) for his own freedom. While examples from Exeter suggest a normative range between two and five shillings (one tenth to one quarter of a pound), a manumission from Bath records that a certain Leofnoth freed himself and his offspring with a sizeable payment of fifty ores, a value three times greater than the pound of silver a thegn holding five hides could expect to make in profit annually.[202] Despite lives of hardship, shaped by relations underpinned by exploitation, some labourers at the lower end of the social spectrum were able to accrue their own surpluses and even become significant figures within the landscape of local politics.

4.4 Guilds

At the confluence between the importance of community, networking, and the potential to promote and inhibit social advancement sits the guild and the guildhall.[203] Guilds took many forms both before and after the Conquest. Unlike the archetypal merchant's guild of the later medieval period, the guilds of the ninth to eleventh centuries (often referred to as gilds to distinguish them from later iterations) were flexible institutions attending to social, economic, and spiritual affairs. Some, such as peace-guilds, were concerned with maintaining law and order while others were strongly linked to churches and emphasised retaining access to burial rites.[204] Socialisation and feasting provided the focal point for many such institutions.[205] They also played a pivotal role in connecting members of the community, with guilds often acting as a form of insurance. Members of the guild were duty bound to protect each other and to pay dues which could act as a method of relief in times of need.[206]

Despite their importance to the functioning of local society, guild statutes rarely form the backbone of scholarly studies. In the seminal collections of 'Anglo-Saxon' primary sources compiled by Benjamin Thorpe and Dorothy

---

[202] Pracy, 'Social Mobility', 18–19. Fleming, 'The New Wealth', 17.

[203] Rosser, 'The Anglo-Saxon Gilds', 31–34; Naismith, "Gilds, States and Societies'.

[204] Epstein, *Wage Labor and Guilds*, 42. Lambert remarks upon the similarities of the London peace-guild and the hundredal system but acknowledges that the guild made no reference to an external power as an official authority within the guild (Lambert, *Law and Order*, 330). For a brief note on their religious connections, see Blair, *The Church in Anglo-Saxon Society*, 453–455. On meeting places more generally and buildings, see Blair, *Building*, 405–408.

[205] Naismith, 'Gilds, States and Societies', 650–651.

[206] Naismith, 'Gilds, States and Societies', 629. On the admittance to guilds and her speculative argument for a relationship between the manumissions and guild records in Exeter, see Treharne, 'The Conners of Exeter', 23–26.

Whitelock, guild statutes were afforded their own, if small, section.[207] Elsewhere, guilds are often namechecked as a phenomenon but largely left out of the conversation.[208] In 1993, Patrick Conner provided a handy study of the physical remains that records the Exeter guilds (i.e., a codicological and palaeographical examination of the *Exeter Book*).[209] More recently, Tom Lambert's monograph considered guilds in greater depth, using them to aid his analysis of the implementation of local order and the application of judicial violence.[210] Studies of this ilk represent the most common scholarly approaches to these records, as a window into social regulation. The work of Duncan Probert has been a notable exception to this pattern of academic research. In 2003, Probert gave a compelling paper – a version of which was published posthumously in 2022 – which unravelled the 'gildship' records of Exeter and suggested that the membership of the Exeter guilds included a significant number of 'peasant farmers'.[211] However, Probert's untimely passing stopped this work in its tracks. Studies by Ann Williams and Rory Naismith in 2016 and 2020 respectively have helped round out our contextual understanding of this corpus of guild records, the latter especially drawing out comparisons between early English and Carolingian associations and their corresponding relationships with state structures.[212] Still, the space that guilds allowed for social competition and the negotiation of social position remains little discussed.[213] This section, therefore, seeks to extend the focus of Probert's work to better establish that the membership of guilds included a wide cross section of low-ranking lay society and consider how they facilitated the construction of rank and status in the period.

The Thegns' Guild at Cambridge is perhaps the most often cited example of these early medieval societies. Given that few guilds clearly indicate who comprised the membership, it is hardly a surprise that this example, which provides some of our clearest data regarding social hierarchy, should draw such attention. The opening of the statutes declares, 'ðæt æle oþrum aþ on haligdome sealde soþre heldrædenne for Gode 7 for worulde. 7 eal geferræden þæm a fylste þe rihtost hæfd' (that each [member] was to give to the others an oath of true loyalty, in regard to religious and secular affairs, on the relics; and all the

---

[207] Thorpe, *Diplomatarium*, 604–617; Whitelock, *EHD I*, 557–560.

[208] Roach, *Kingship and Consent*, 109, 118.   [209] Conner, *Anglo-Saxon Exeter*.

[210] Lambert, *Law and Order*, 154, 182, 209, 214, 228–230, 247, 301, 315, 330–332, 353. Lambert only made use of two guild statutes: V Æthelstan and the Thegns' Guild of Cambridge.

[211] Probert, 'Exeter's Gildship and Manumission Records'.

[212] Williams, 'A Place in the Country'; Naismith, 'Gilds, States and Societies'.

[213] Alban Gautier's chapter addresses this issue tangentially, but his work focuses upon the egalitarian language of the guild statutes, and he argues that these ideals did not manifest in the day-to-day practices of the guildhall (Gautier, 'Discours égalitaire et pratiques hiérarchques').

fellowship was ever to aid him who had most right).[214] The guild guaranteed that members would: receive help if a crime was committed against them or if they justly slew someone outside the guild; provide aid if a blood-feud ensued; attend the body of a dying or deceased guild member; retrieve a guild member or their corpse if they had fallen ill or passed away some distance from their own lands; and ensure that fallen guild members would be remembered via a large funeral feast. This seemingly forged a strong horizontal connection between guild members, who could easily focus their thegnly identity through this collective and thus effectively enact a form of social closure. Still, things may be a little more complicated than they initially appear.

While the source carefully identifies that each guild brother was to contribute two ores towards the compensation for the killing of a ceorlish non-member, it also notes that each guild brother was to provide half a mark if the victim was a man with a wergild of 1,200 shillings. Thus, we are presented with two possibilities: (a) that the man with a wergild of 1,200 shillings was a thegnly non-member or (b) that he was neither defined by his thegnliness nor ceorlishness, but solely by his wergild. The former would imply that the Thegns' Guild at Cambridge, which expressly describes itself in these terms, was not some entity of which all thegns in the region were members. Although the association may have operated as a way for some thegns to stress their collective rank and exclude those without, it is even possible that non-thegnly individuals were allowed entry as long as they were someone's retainer. Even more pressing is the likelihood that that there were numerous thegns who did not partake in this attempt to separate themselves from other ranks in this way. Given the location of the guild in the Danelaw, it may also be that the thegnliness held relatively little weight and that it was a title that could be adopted by anyone who was free.[215] This prospect perhaps lends credence to the latter possibility, that the man with a 1,200 shilling wergild is not necessarily a thegn or a ceorl. Returning to the apparent discrepancies in the application of wergilds highlighted in Section 2, it may be that the term ceorl is functioning here as a shorthand for a certain wergild and a legal rank rather than a social rank.[216] By comparison, the term *thegn* may be operating as a social rank rather than defining their legal position. Whatever the case may be, the members of the Thegns' Guild at Cambridge evidently sought to separate themselves from other lay members of society, stressing the fidelity to one another and excluding others from enjoying their 'geferes 7 freondscipes' (society and friendship).[217]

Other elites, to borrow a turn of phrase from Patrick Wormald, did not merely write themselves into the activities of a guild but sought to reorchestrate the

---

[214] Thorpe, *Diplomatarium*, 610.   [215] Stattel, 'Legal Culture in the Danelaw', 201.

[216] See discussion concerning how we may define a ceorl in Section 2.

[217] Whitelock, *EHD I*, 558.

entire symphony of guild behaviour in a key set by the founder.[218] The Guild of Urk/Ork (also known as the Guild at Abbotsbury) offers an example of one such individual:

> Her cyð on þisum gewrite þ Orcy hæfð gegyfen þæ gegyldhealle 7 þone stede æt Abbodesbyrig Gode to lofe 7 S[an]c[t]e Petre. 7 þam gyldscipe to agenne. on dæge 7 æfter dæge. him 7 his gebeddan to langsumum gemynde.

> Here it is made known in this document that Urki has given the guildhall and the site at Abbotsbury to the praise of God and St. Peter and for the guildship to own in his lifetime and after it, in lasting memory of himself and his wife.[219]

Crucially, it is possible to locate this individual in other documents and identify his rank. Urk was a locally important individual in mid eleventh-century Dorset, who was the beneficiary of a writ issued by Edward the Confessor between 1053 and 1058:

> Eadward kingc gret Alfwold b. 7 Harold eorl and Alfred scyrgereuan. and ealle mine þegenes on Dorsætan freondlice. 7 ic ciþe eow þ Urk min huskarl habbe his strand eall forne gen hys agen land ofer eal wel 7 feolice. upp of sæ 7 ut on sæ. 7 eall þ to his strande gedryuen hys. Be minum fullan bebode.

> I, King Edward, greet bishop Ælfwold, and earl Harold, and Ælfred shire-reeve, and all my thegns in Dorsetshire, amicably. And I make known to you that Urk, my huscarl, may have his shore, all in front of his own land, over well and freely, up from sea and out on sea, and all that is driven to his shore, by my full command.[220]

Urk was not only a huscarl to royalty but was also in possession of lucrative rights to control the shoreline and sea abutting his property. Urk held additional property at Portesham and Abbott's Wootton, granted to him by Cnut in 1024 and Edward in 1044 respectively.[221] The sizes of his smaller estates are readily identifiable: Portesham was held at eleven and three quarter hides; Abbott's Wootton was assessed at only two and a half hides. Abbotsbury, which appears to have been Urk's primary residence, was a large estate measured at twenty-two hides.[222] Urk's wife, Tole, likely held another eighteen hides at Tolpuddle in her own right.[223] There are more variables that may have affected the size of his property portfolio than can be addressed here. Nonetheless, it is not controversial

---

[218] For the original quote discussing the regulation of feuding, see Wormald, 'Giving God and King Their Due', 341.

[219] Thorpe, *Diplomatarium*, 604.   [220] S1063 in Thorpe, *Diplomatarium*, 414.

[221] Whitelock, *EHD I*, 559.   [222] Williams, 'A Place in the Country'.

[223] Whitelock, *EHD I*, 559.

to say that Urk and his wife controlled close to forty hides. This would have placed him among some of the wealthiest individuals in the kingdom and might even have numbered among the *proceres* (chief men) or *optimates* (best men) described in some sources.[224]

It is hard to precisely date the gift of the guildhall and the recording of its statutes, but we may presume that the guildhall was gifted sometime after Urk began to acquire serious property in 1024 and before 1066, when a charter records that Tole, now described as his widow, alienated land at Abbotsbury.[225] It would appear he was the architect of the guild and the location of the hall in his land allowed the guild to serve as a vehicle for the expression of his local importance. Unlike other examples, we do not know much about the member-ship of the guild itself. However, we can perhaps speculate regarding the benefits that this guild provided Urk. All guild members had to travel to Urk's own estate – entering his space at his invitation – and bear witness to the wealth displayed within his guildhall. Existing at the apex of the hierarchy of the guild, Urk's later gift functioned as an act of memorialisation 'in lasting memory of himself and his wife'.[226] He was both master of the space in which the guild met and its lasting benefactor. All who trod the earth of his guildhall were made debtors to his generosity. The life cycle of this guild and its guildhall was shaped by the legacy of Urk and his status within local society.

Beyond memorialisation, the guildhall may have helped to increase Urk's social prestige by cementing him as a potential lord. In the latter half of the eleventh century, there appears to have been an increase in the level of competi-tion among lords. Analyses of surveys and the like, such as the *Domesday Book*, reveal 'that it was usual for several different lords to have interests in any particular locality' and thus a lord would find it challenging to monopolize judicial proceedings in the area.[227] Consequently, though lords wished to shape vertical relationships in their favour, there were some practical limits. Indeed, the record of commendation practices (the swearing of an oath of loyalty to a lord in exchange for protection) in the *Domesday Book* 'demonstrates the existence of competition between lords for commendations in many localities.[228] In short, while a good number of freemen were subservient to a lord in a tenurial sense, they also seem – at least at the end of our period – to have sought out a lord to whom they might owe allegiance and who they believed could advocate for them effectively at the local court. At the same time, some lords were building up a base

---

[224] Clarke, *The English Nobility under Edward the Confessor*, 34n4.

[225] 'Urces lafe' (Thorpe, *Diplomatarium*, 576).

[226] 'His gebeddan to langsumum gemynde' (Thorpe, *Diplomatarium*, 604; Whitelock, *EHD I*, 559).

[227] Baxter, 'Lordship and Justice', 388.   [228] Baxter, 'Lordship and Justice', 418.

of social influence by seeking to establish as many commendations as possible. Urk's position as the patron of the guild would have certainly allowed him to construct something of a pipeline, permitting him to acquire as many commendations as he wished. Given the late date of this gift of the guildhall, this may well not have entered Urk's mind, but it is possible to speculate that such activities occurred elsewhere. Accordingly, guilds may have allowed aspirants to rapidly increase their social standing.

Though guilds could be dominated by thegnly elites, as in the previous examples, many guilds, or at least those in the Devon, had diverse memberships. Only those who were unfree seem to have been wholly excluded from holding membership of these guilds, and even this may have been more down to means than social stigma.[229] Indeed, membership was something that one had to maintain, both fiscally and socially. The guild statutes of the Thegns' Guild at Cambridge and the Guild of Urk make it quite clear that annual dues were an essential component of retaining membership and access to these associations, regardless of any other barriers.[230] Through remarkable fortune, the Exeter Book records the names of 304 members of fourteen guilds in the hinterlands surrounding the city and provides a window into the composition of the guilds of the South West. Though what remains preserves only traces of post-Conquest guilds, several of the members can be identified as being active landholders during King Harold's ill-fated reign.[231] What emerges when the guild lists are cross-referenced with the Domesday surveys is a notable similarity between the two records, with the population of the vills (an administrative unit comparable to a parish) in the Domesday survey, from villein to bordar, aligning in many instances with the members listed in the guild records. Some of these members can also be confidently identified as lords of the related vill, such as Ailsi (likely a Latinised form of the Old English name Ælfsige) who held in total about two and a half hides in Doddiscombsleigh and Lowley.[232] Lords were invested in these localised guilds and seemingly partook in their activities. The guild lists of the Exeter Book were, presumably, carefully updated to reflect who the cathedral could expect to receive renders from and to whom they owed their spiritual services. Establishing precedence may not, however, have been as straightforward as one might think. Returning to Ælfsige, lord of Doddiscombsleigh, it is worth noting that he was not placed at the head of the records for the associated

---

[229] Naismith, 'Gilds, States and Societies', 655–656; Pracy, '"Medeman mannum"', 158–165.

[230] Thorpe, *Diplomatarium*, 605–608, 610–613; See also Naismith, 'Gilds, States and Societies', 653–656.

[231] Duncan Probert was the first to begin cross-referencing the Domesday data with the guild records in earnest, but his work was cut short by his untimely death. See Probert, 'Exeter's Gildship and Manumission Records'.

[232] Pracy, '"Medeman mannum"', 160–161.

guild. Instead, that honour went to individuals who cannot be securely tied to immediate area.[233] Where numbers exceed those recorded in the Domesday data, it may benefit us to acknowledge the possibility that guild members were members of multiple such associations. If so, this would represent numerous interlocking local communities, predominantly comprised by non-nobles. In short, some aspiring and well-to-do families of the region may have used their surpluses to finance the maintenance of several memberships in different guilds, viewing the networking possibilities as a worthwhile investment.

The presence of these kinds of associations in the everyday fabric of rural society and the upwardly mobile who they may well have served is supported by the distribution of so-called prestige objects (objects which served to indicate status). These items do not offer an entirely conclusive image, especially given that artefacts surviving from tenth-century rural settlements are hard to utilise as indicators of the status of sites.[234] Moreover, earlier evidence from the eighth and early ninth centuries shows the presence of a range of prestige objects in non-elite rural settlements, while later survivals in rural settlements commonly include only coins and equestrian equipment.[235] This latter category of equipment – such as the copper-alloy elements which comprised part of key equestrian equipment, including the stirrups, harness, and bridle – are widely found into the eleventh century and may well be part of the 'standard' equipment of non-noble elites such as *rædmaen* or *geneats*.[236] This is, perhaps, the material legacy of the kinds of aspirational social actors who jockeyed for position in local guilds.

The importance of local guilds in the tenth and eleventh centuries appears to reflect other demographic changes in the period, such as the increasing urbanisation of the region. To be sure, rural activities overwhelmingly shaped the majority of the lives of those dwelling in England. Yet towns and cities saw an increase in their populations and associated professions, such as merchants. The guilds and associated practices discussed in this section, especially those enacted in the environs of Exeter, seem to have penetrated quite far into the hinterlands of the city. The connectedness of cities to their surrounding populations should be of no surprise at this point in time, especially given that many thegns who lived outside of urban areas held sizeable interests in urban plots.[237] If we turn to a quite different area of England, the East Midlands, we find that lords were not only invested in holding profitable land inside the city of Lincoln, but also founded

---

[233] Pracy, '"Medeman mannum"', 161.   [234] Lewis, *Pattern and Process*, 244–246.

[235] Lewis, *Pattern and Process*, 157–160, 244–246.

[236] Webley, 'Conquests and Continuity', 406. See also Weikert, 'Of Pots and Pins'; Hinton, 'Demography', 152.

[237] Fleming, 'Rural Elites and Urban Communities', 3–19.

churches to suit the needs of their tenants.[238] Moreover, trade was becoming so lucrative in some cities that churches were founded on market squares, presumably not only to provide spiritual services but also to offer other amenities related to mercantile activity, including the swearing of oaths, the scribing and witnessing of documents, the storing of money, and a place to gather.[239] Not content to just display their wealth in life, there are even signs that mercantile elites were using their newfound riches to purchase opulent grave markers, thus signalling their social status.[240] Of course, the East Midlands, featuring a strong Scandinavian influence, are quite some distance from the South West, and it may well be that certain regions were experiencing change in divergent ways and differing degrees. The heartlands of Wessex may well have exhibited a vertical hierarchy that was more resilient compared to other regions. Still, the overall trend across England appears to have been one of increased social competition at the middle and lower points of the social spectrum, one that continued well into the fading of the eleventh century. Hence, Christopher Loveluck's observation that 'it becomes very difficult to distinguish a town-house of a landed aristocrat from a town-house of a rich merchant-patrician' by the early twelfth century.[241]

Guilds acted as a vector for various forms of social exclusion and social mobility. One can well imagine that, if faced with a financial surplus, someone might choose to invest in cementing their membership across multiple guilds, thus broadening their networking horizons. Although allegedly taking place towards the end of the eleventh century, the events recorded in the *Life of Christina of Markyate* are suggestive of the ways that aspirational (mercantile) freemen may have been tempted to utilise such spaces to improve the fortunes of their families, namely brokering favourable marriage agreements.[242] Moreover, there are also strong indications that bringing retainers or associates to such events was an expected part of a guild members' behaviour.[243] This was done perhaps to not only demonstrate to other members the impressive retinue that one might be able to muster, but also as a reward, both in terms of the material experience and the networking opportunities it might offer. A crude comparison may be to think of the space as something akin to a highly exclusive golf-club, where lavish functions are held, social jostling takes place, and business deals

---

[238] Stocker, 'Aristocrats, Burghers and Their Markets', 139.

[239] Stocker, 'Aristocrats, Burghers and Their Markets', 139–140.

[240] Stocker, 'Monuments and Merchants', 206–207.

[241] Loveluck, *Northwest Europe in the Early Middle Ages*, 366–367.

[242] Talbot, *The Life of Christina of Markyate*, 54.

[243] The Thegns' Guild at Cambridge allowed someone to be accompanied into the *stig* by a retainer for a levy of one sester of honey sit and, for the same amount, they might be accompanied by a *fotsetla*. See Thorpe, *Diplomatarium*, 612.

are hashed out.[244] Of course, just as such avenues may have helped improve a family's standing, guilds were also potential venues for preventing the rise of the nouveaux riches and practising forms of social exclusion. Even the Exeter guild lists, which hint at diverse membership patterns, objectivised the membership of these associations on parchment, expressly defining who was 'in' and who was 'out', especially if they could not afford their annual dues. (The golf-club analogy perhaps lends itself neatly here too.) Thus guilds had the potential to both temporarily solidify what was often a plastic social hierarchy and permit its remoulding.

5 Conclusion

Returning to a quote taken from the work of Christine Senecal, she states: 'no single characteristic, or set of characteristics, prescribed who did or did not have aristocratic status in late Anglo-Saxon England'.[245] As noted, I agree with the broad sentiment. For the inhabitants of early medieval England, there was no one-size-fits-all approach to defining thegnly rank nor, indeed, other ranks. By looking at variously ranked people – especially thegns and ceorls – across early medieval English society, this Element has shown that it is possible to identify a broad range of characteristics which served to delimit who was and who was not considered a thegn (or thegnly). These characteristics or their representational components acted as a loose benchmark. Those who cleared certain representational thresholds were taken by observers to be what they appeared, with thegnliness being a particularly salient example and an especially desirable aim for aspiring ceorls. A key aspect of this, however, is that not *all* thegns were necessarily able to display *all* of these characteristics while some ceorls could more successfully do so despite not having the same social claim to the rank. Beyond the thegnhood, those who held any particular rank did not form a homogenous group, but rather comprised a whole host of heterogeneous individuals who were loosely linked through a wide web of partially shared characteristics. It is evident that there were further, though less obvious, subdivisions within early medieval English society based upon articulations of lineage and other differentiators. Even the political commentators of early medieval England, such as Wulfstan, recognised the need to employ a range of methods to describe the complexities of the social landscape in which they found themselves.

---

[244] My knowledge of such spaces is anecdotal rather than based upon intimate knowledge. If I have erred in my understanding of such spaces, I hope, at least, that the comparison still bears some fruit.

[245] Senecal, 'Keeping Up with the Godwinesons', 251.

In the case of the thegnhood, the non-institutional honorific that was the rank of thegn did not necessarily confer any legal or social benefits on its own. It did, however, suggest to an observer several qualities that the bearer of the title was likely to possess. As a term, it was able to confer prestige upon someone to whom the title was bestowed. This is why the rank of thegn retained social currency, remaining ubiquitous across narrative and dispositive sources despite not being linked to concrete benefits and why there are hints that aspirants would have desired the rank.

Considering the broader issues of social status at hand, one key takeaway from the argument here is that although the routes to gaining status were many and varied, there were, of course, those who sought to curtail access through any means at their disposal. For example, we find many instances where middling people – whether thegn or ceorl – sought to stress the value of their rank: during mass in the local church; at the meeting of the hundredal court; at the annual ritual of beating the bounds; or when they witnessed charters. Across all these moments in time, their social position was in flux, constantly in a state of renegotiation and in need of recognition (at least by certain persons deemed socially important). Underpinning these performances, of course, is that not everyone had access to the same identities. This is the coal that fuels the engine of differentiation and stratification. Thus, for some, the title of thegn was enough to encourage collectivization. Hence, the Thegns' Guild at Cambridge proved a viable option for those seeking to more firmly demarcate social boundaries and keep out would-be thegns. For others, rank does not appear to have been key to their self-perception or how they were recognised by others in the sources. Rather, other qualities were stressed in such instances, presumably because it granted them more prestige in a specific social context. In short, rank was simply one aspect of many that formed an individual's identity, and which helped to cement a person's overall status in society.

Occupations, such as moneyers or merchants, stretched across the boundaries of rank, and perhaps fostered different forms of social affiliation.[246] Officials, such as reeves or even village beadles, may have held less land than their neighbours, but enjoyed a greater degree of local influence due to their position of authority.[247] Bridging these categories, it was entirely possible that priests

---

[246] On lowlier 'professional' and wealthier 'gentlemen' moneyers, see Naismith, 'The Moneyers and Domesday Book', 194–195. On merchants, see Fleming, 'Rural Elites and Urban Communities', 17, 33–36.

[247] On the varied duties fulfilled and rewards received by reeves, see Williams, *The World before Domesday*, 81–100. Note her discussion of 'reevelands'. For the variety of holdings enjoyed by beadles, see GDB BED 25,12; 57,3v; 57,17 & 57,18; GDB CAMB 1,20.

might function as merchants, moneyers, reeves, and thegns.[248] While others fulfilled roles typically understood to have been less prestigious, such as that of the shepherd, in some cases such individuals seem to have possessed more land than their neighbours who performed ostensibly more lucrative professions.[249] Intersecting with all such vectors by which status was constructed were the practices of patronage and commendation. An individual who found a wealthy and powerful advocate could find their social position quickly elevated. Therefore, while rank played an important role in determining the hierarchy of early medieval England, there were numerous aspects that all served to influence the stratification of society.

The ranks of early medieval England cannot, therefore, act as a secure guide to social precedence. Nor, indeed, can they convey with any certainty the means and benefits that someone bearing these titles necessarily enjoyed. If we are to improve clarity in the field, a more robust approach is needed moving forward. I suggest that compound descriptors, such as lordly ceorls/thegns, ceorlish reeves, or dependent thegns, would be beneficial when describing the relative social statuses of those in our sources. These would allow us to better describe our poorer thegns, fallen on hard times and who had become dependent on another's patronage and support in court. Moreover, it would help us to separate our exploited ceorlish peasants from our lordly ceorls, who sought to rise up the social ladder and behaved in ways more typically associated with thegnhood.

All of this serves not to gloss over the harsh realities of how power was constructed nor how many in the countryside laboured under strict limits imposed by someone else. The lives of ceorls could be, and often were, dominated and shaped by seigneurial exploitation and violence. Certain sources do seem to reinforce the idea of a monolithic and indivisible ceorlish rank. However, such seeming homogeneity in the period regarding rank related terms is, I suggest, the product of a scribal tendency to flatten social hierarchies, erasing potentialities for confusion and streamlining the objectivization of these groups on the page. It is entirely within the bounds of possibility that such distinctions were deliberate attempts to curtail social mobility. Yet, more often than not, it is largely that the types of sources which survive in significant numbers focused upon qualities which could be best linked to rank. Beyond the handy, if thin, signifier of rank, scribes do not seem to have often cared to record other dimensions of social stratification.

Viewing darkly the society of early medieval England through terse scribal lenses, scholars have understandably followed such distinctions. Yet, by making

---

[248] Naismith, 'The Moneyers and Domesday Book', 195. See also Blair, *The Church in Anglo-Saxon Society*, 491–492.

[249] See Section 3.

use of a more robust framework, we may be able to more securely understand the intricacies of social hierarchy in the period. It may, of course, be true to say that it is impossible to avoid using terminology which simplifies and obfuscates the complexities and multivalency of social interaction. Are we not all bound by the same unescapable, conceptual constrictions? Nonetheless, it may be our role as historians to find those options that help illuminate the past as much as possible. By collectively favouring terminology that centres the multiplicity of experiences, we can move towards a fuller vision of inequality and hierarchy in early medieval England. Returning, at last, to the madder-keeper, swineherd, and dairymaid, all of whom were transferred so easily by the religious institution at Ely, it is necessary to note that all had complex lives not solely defined by the simple designators which the medieval scribe or the historian chooses to ascribe to them. In each moment, in each venue, their experience differed and so did the relationality they negotiated with those above, below, and beside them.

Abbreviations

Af.	Laws of Alfred (See Jurasinski and Oliver)
At.	Laws of Æthelstan (See Liebermann)
Atr.	Laws of Æthelred (See Liebermann)
Bodmin	London, British Library, MS. Royal 1.Bvii, MS. Add. 9381 (See Förster)
Cn.	Laws of Cnut (See Liebermann)
Em.	Laws of Edmund (See Liebermann)
GDB	*Greater Domesday Book.* Cited by county and Phillimore reference. For example, 'GDB CORN 4,17' would indicate *Domesday Book*, vol. 6, Cornwall, ed. by F. Thorn and C. Thorn (Chichester: Phillimore, 1979), §4,17.
Ine	Laws of Ine (See Jurasinski and Oliver)
Leofric Missal	Oxford, Bodleian Library, Bodley 579 (See Earle)
MED	*Middle English Dictionary*
OED	*Oxford English Dictionary*
RSP	*Rectitudines singularum personarum* (See Gobbitt)
S	Pre-Conquest charters are referred to by their 'Sawyer numbers'.

Bibliography

Abels, Richard P., *Lordship and Military Obligation in Anglo-Saxon England* (Berkeley: University of California Press, 1988).

Assman, Bruno, ed., *Angelsächsische Homilien und Heiligenleben* (Kassel, DE: G. H. Wigand, 1889).

Aston, Mick, and Christopher Gerrard, *Interpreting the English Village: Landscape and Community at Shapwick, Somerset* (Oxford: Oxbow Books, 2013).

Banham, Debbie, *Food and Drink in Anglo-Saxon England* (Stroud, UK: Tempus, 2004).

Barthélemy, Dominique, *The Serf, the Knight, and the Historian*, ed. and trans. by G. R. Edwards (Ithaca, NY: Cornell University Press, 2009).

Bates, David, ed., *Regesta Regum Anglo-Normannorum: The Acts of William I (1066–1087)* (Oxford: Clarendon, 1998).

Baxter, Stephen, 'Archbishop Wulfstan and the Administration of God's Property', in Matthew Townend (ed.), *Wulfstan, Archbishop of York: The Proceedings of the Second Alcuin Conference* (Turnhout: Brepols, 2004), 161–205.

'Lordship and Justice in the Early English Kingdom: The Judicial Functions of Soke and Commendation Revisited', in Stephen Baxter, Catherine Karkov, Janet Nelson, and David Pelteret (eds.), *Early Medieval Studies in Memory of Patrick Wormald* (Farnham: Ashgate 2009), 383–420.

Baxter, Stephen, and John Blair, 'Land Tenure and Royal Patronage in the Early English Kingdom: A Model and Case Study', *Anglo-Norman Studies* 28 (2006), 19–46.

Bethurum, Dorothy, 'Archbishop Wulfstan's Commonplace Book', *PMLA* 57 (1942), 916–929.

The Homilies of Wulfstan (Oxford: Clarendon, 1957).

'Six Anonymous Old English Codes', *Journal of English and Germanic Philology*, 49 (1950), 449–463.

Blair, John, *Building Anglo-Saxon England* (Princeton, NJ: Princeton University Press, 2018).

The Church in Anglo-Saxon Society (Oxford: Oxford University Press, 2005).

'The Limits of Bookland', *Anglo-Saxon England* 48 (2022), 197–252.

Bosworth, Joseph, *An Anglo-Saxon Dictionary: Based on the Manuscript Collections of the Late Joseph Bosworth*, ed. by E. N. Toller (Oxford: Clarendon, 1898).

Bougard, François, Geneviève Bührer-Thierry, and Régine Le Jan, 'Elites in the Early Middle Ages: Identities, Strategies, Mobility', *Annales: Histoire, Sciences, Sociales*, trans. by Katharine Throssell, 68 (2013), 735–768.

Cambridge University Library, MS Mm. iv.19.

Campbell, James, 'The Sale of Land and the Economics of Power in Early England: Problems and Possibilities', *Haskins Society Journal*, 1 (1989), 23–37.

'Some Agents and Agencies of the Late Anglo-Saxon State', in *Anglo-Saxon History* (London: Bloomsbury, 2000), 201–225.

Campbell, James, Eric John, and Patrick Wormald, *The Anglo-Saxons* (Oxford: Phaidon, 1982).

Carnicelli, T. A., ed., *King Alfred's Version of St Augustine's Soliloquies* (Cambridge, MA: Harvard University Press, 1969).

Chambers, R. W., Max Förster, and Robin Flower, eds., *The Exeter Book of Old English Poetry* (London: For the Dean and Chapter of Exeter Cathedral by P. Lund, Humphries & Company, Ltd, 1933).

Clarke, Peter A., *The English Nobility under Edward the Confessor* (Oxford: Clarendon, 1994).

Clayton, Mary, '*De Duodecim Abusiuis*: Lordship and Kingship in Anglo-Saxon England', in Stuart McWilliams (ed.), *Saints and Scholars: New Perspectives on Anglo-Saxon Literature and Culture in Honour of Hugh Magennis* (Woodbridge: D. S. Brewer, 2012), 141–163.

Colgrave, Bertram, and R. A. B. Mynors, eds. and trans., *Bede's Ecclesiastical History of the English People* (Oxford: Oxford University Press, 1969).

Conner, Patrick W., *Anglo-Saxon Exeter: A Tenth-Century Cultural History* (Woodbridge: Boydell, 1993).

Constable, Giles, *Three Studies in Medieval and Religious & Social Thought* (Cambridge: Cambridge University Press, 1995).

Coss, Peter R., *The Aristocracy in England and Tuscany, 1000–1250* (Oxford: Oxford University Press, 2019).

Crouch, David, *The Birth of Nobility. Constructing Aristocracy in England and France: 900–1300* (London: Pearson Education, 2005).

The English Aristocracy 1070–1272: A Social Transformation (New Haven, CT: Yale University Press, 2011).

Cubitt, Catherine, '"As the Lawbook Teaches": Reeves, Lawbooks and Urban Life in the Anonymous Old English Legend of the Seven Sleepers', *English Historical Review*, 124 (2009), 1021–1049.

Day, Emma, 'Sokemen and Freemen in Late Anglo-Saxon East Anglia in Comparative Context', unpublished PhD thesis, University of Cambridge (2011).

Divjak, Dagmar, and Antti Arppe, 'Extracting Prototypes from Exemplars: What Can Corpus Data Tell Us about Concept Representation', *Cognitive Linguistics*, 24 (2013), 221–274.

Douglas, D. C., ed., *Feudal Documents from the Abbey of Bury St. Edmunds* (London: British Academy and Oxford University Press, 1932).

Dresch, Paul, 'Legalism, Anthropology, and History: A View from Part of Anthropology', in Paul Dresch and Hannah Skoda (eds.), *Legalism* (Oxford: Oxford University Press, 2012), 1–13.

Duby, Georges, *The Three Orders: Feudal Society Imagined*, trans. by Arthur Goldhammer (Chicago, IL: University of Chicago Press, 1982).

Earle, John, *A Hand-Book to the Land-Charters and Other Saxonic Documents* (Oxford: Clarendon, 1888).

Epstein, S. A., *Wage Labor and Guilds in Medieval Europe* (Chapel Hill: University of North Carolina Press, 1991).

Escalona, Julio, 'Dense Local Knowledge: Grounding Local to Supralocal Relationships in Tenth-Century Castille', in Julio Escalona, Orri Vésteinsson, and Stuart Brookes (eds.), *Polity and Neighbourhood in Early Medieval Europe* (Turnhout: Brepols, 2019), 351–379.

'Territorialidad e identidades locales en la Castilla condal', in José Antonio Jara Fuente, Georges Martin, and Isabel Alfonso (eds.), *Construir la identidad en la Edad Media* (Cuenca: Universidad de Castilla–La Mancha, 2010), 55–82.

Fairweather, Janet, ed. and trans., *Liber Eliensis: A History of the Isle of Ely from the Seventh Century to the Twelfth* (Woodbridge: Boydell, 2005).

Faith, Rosamond, *The English Peasantry and the Growth of Lordship* (London: Leicester University Press, 1997).

The Moral Economy of the Countryside: Anglo-Saxon to Anglo-Norman England (Cambridge: Cambridge University Press, 2019).

'Tidenham, Gloucestershire, and the History of the Manor in England', *Landscape History*, 16 (1994), 39–51.

Fleming, Robin, 'Rural Elites and Urban Communities in Late-Saxon England', *Past & Present*, 141 (1993), 3–37.

'The New Wealth, the New Rich and the New Political Style in Late Anglo-Saxon England', *Anglo-Norman Studies*, 23 (2001), 1–22.

Flight, Tim, 'Aristocratic Deer Hunting in Late Anglo-Saxon England: A Reconsideration, Based Upon the *Vita S. Dvnstani*', *Anglo-Saxon England*, 45 (2017), 311–331.

Förster, Max, 'Die Freilassungsurkunden des Bodmin-Evangeliars', in Niels Bøgholm, A. Brusendorff, and C. A. Bodelsen (eds.), *A Grammatical*

Miscellany Offered to Otto Jespersen on His Seventieth Birthday (London: Allen and Unwin, 1930), 77–99.

Freedman, Paul, *Images of the Medieval Peasant* (Stanford, CA: Stanford University Press, 1999).

Galbraith, V. H., 'An Episcopal Land-Grant of 1085', *English Historical Review*, 44 (1939), 353–372.

Gautier, Alban, 'Discours égalitaire et pratiques hiérarchques dans les guildes anglo-saxonnes', in Dominique Iogna-Prat, François Bougard, and Régine Le Jan (eds.), *Hiérarchie et stratification sociale dans l'Occident medieval 400–1100* (Turnhout: Brepols, 2008), 343–362.

Gillingham, John, 'Thegns and Knights in Eleventh-Century England: Who Was Then the Gentleman?', *Transactions of the Royal Historical Society*, 6 (5) (1995), 129–154.

Gobbitt, Thom, ed. and trans., *Gerefa (RSP+ Ger)*, https://earlyenglishlaws.ac.uk/laws/texts/rspger/view/#edition/commentary-3.

Godden, Malcolm R., 'Money, Power and Morality in Late Anglo-Saxon England', *Anglo-Saxon England*, 19 (1990), 41–65.

Gurevich, Aaron J., 'Medieval Culture and Mentality According to the New French Historiography', *Archives Européennes de Sociologie*, 24(1983), 183–195.

Hadley, D. M., *The Northern Danelaw: Its Social Structure, c.800–1100* (London: Leicester University Press, 2000).

Harvey, Paul, 'Rectitudines Singularum Personarum and Gerefa', *English Historical Review*, 426 (1993), 1–22.

Higham, Robert, 'The Godwins, Towns and St Olaf Churches: Comital Investment in the Mid-11th Century', in Alexander Langlands and Ryan Lavelle (eds.), *The Land of The English Kin: Studies in Wessex and Anglo-Saxon England in Honour of Professor Barbara Yorke* (Leiden: Brill, 2020), 467–513.

Hilton, Rodney, 'Medieval Peasants: Any Lessons?', in *Class Conflict and the Crisis of Feudalism: Essays in Medieval Social History* (London: Bloomsbury, 1985), 114–121.

'Reasons for Inequality among Medieval Peasants', in *Class Conflict and the Crisis of Feudalism: Essays in Medieval Social History* (London: Bloomsbury, 1985), 139–151.

Hinton, David, 'Demography: From Domesday and Beyond', *Journal of Medieval History*, 39 (2013), 146–178.

Hooke, Della, *The Landscape of Anglo-Saxon England* (London: Leicester University Press, 1998).

Hudson, John, *The Oxford History of the Laws of England: 871–1216*, vol. 2 (Oxford: Oxford University Press, 2012).

Hyams, Paul, 'Servitude in Anglo-Saxon England: Searching for the Serfs', in Stefan Jurasinski and Andrew Rabin (eds.), *Languages of the Law in Early Medieval England: Essays in Memory of Lisi Oliver* (Leuven:Peeters, 2019), 127–153.

Insley, Charles, 'Assemblies and Charters in Late Anglo-Saxon England', in P. Barnwell and M. Mostert (eds.), *Political Assemblies in the Earlier Middle Ages* (Turnhout: Brepols, 2003), 47–59.

'Kings and Lords in Tenth-Century Cornwall', *History*, 98 (2013), 2–22.

Jurasinski, Stefan, and Lisi Oliver, *The Laws of Alfred: The Domboc and the Making of Anglo-Saxon Law* (Cambridge: Cambridge University Press, 2021).

Keynes, Simon, 'Mercia and Wessex in the Ninth Century', in M. P. Brown and C. A. Farr (eds.), *Mercia: An Anglo-Saxon Kingdom in Europe* (London: Leicester University Press, 2001), 310–328.

Keynes, Simon, and A. Kennedy, ed. and trans., *The Libellus Æthelwoldi Episcopi* (Oxford: British Academy and Royal Historical Society Joint Committee on Anglo-Saxon Charters, forthcoming).

Keynes, Simon, and Michael Lapidge, ed. and trans., *Alfred the Great: Asser's Life of King Alfred and Other Contemporary Sources* (London: Penguin Books, 1983).

King, Vanessa, 'St. Oswald's Tenants', in Nicholas Brooks and Catherine Cubitt (eds.), *St Oswald: Life and Influence* (London: Leicester, 1996), 100–116.

Koziol, Geoffrey, *The Peace of God* (Kalamazoo, MI: ARC Humanities, 2018).

Lakoff, George, *Women, Fire, and Dangerous Things: What Categories Reveal about the Mind* (Chicago, IL: University of Chicago Press, 1987).

Lambert, Tom, *Law and Order in Anglo-Saxon England* (Oxford: Oxford University Press, 2017).

Langlands, Alexander, 'Local Places and Local People: Peasant Agency and the Formation of the Anglo-Saxon State', in Julio Escalona, Orri Vésteinsson, and Stuart Brookes (eds.), *Polity and Neighbourhood in Early Medieval Europe* (Turnhout: Brepols, 2019), 381–405.

Lavelle, Ryan, *Alfred's Wars: Sources and Interpretations of Anglo-Saxon Warfare in the Viking Age* (Woodbridge: Boydell Press, 2010).

Lawson, M. K., *Cnut: The Danes in England in the Early Eleventh Century* (New York: Longman, 1993).

Lemanski, S. Jay, 'Slave or Free: The Æhtemann in Anglo-Saxon England', *Haskins Society Journal*, 29 (2017), 53–80.

Lewis, Christopher P., 'Domesday Jurors', *Haskins Society Journal*, 5 (1993), 17–44.

Lewis, Hana, *Pattern and Process in the Material Culture of Anglo-Saxon Non-elite Rural Settlements* (Oxford: British Archaeological Reports, 2019).

Leyser, Conrad, 'Introduction: The Transformation of Law in the Late and Post-Roman World', *Early Medieval Europe*, 27 (2019), 5–11.

Liebermann, Felix, ed. and trans., *Die Gesetze der Angelsachsen*, vol. 1 (Halle: Max Niemeyer, 1903–16).

Loveluck, Christopher, *Northwest Europe in the Early Middle Ages, 600–1150: A Comparative Archaeology* (Cambridge: Cambridge University Press, 2013).

Lowe, Kathryn, 'The Development of the Anglo-Saxon Boundary Clause', *Nomina*, 11 (1998), 63–100.

Loyn, Henry R., 'Gesith and Thegns in Anglo-Saxon England from the Seventh to the Tenth Century', *English Historical Review*, 70 (1955), 529–549.

Machery, Edouard, 'A Better Philosophy for a Better Psychology: Comment on Slaney and Racine', *Journal of Theoretical and Philosophical Psychology*, 31 (2011), 90–95.

McClain, Aleksandra, and Naomi Sykes, 'New Archaeologies of the Norman Conquest', *Anglo-Norman Studies*, 41 (2019), 83–101.

Margolis, Eric, and Stephen Laurence, *Concepts: Core Readings* (Cambridge, MA: MIT Press, 1999).

Middle English Compendium. University of Michigan. https://quod.lib.umich .edu/m/middle-english-dictionary/dictionary.

Medin, Douglas L., and Marguerite M. Schaffer, 'Context Theory of Classification Learning', *Psychology Review*, 85 (1978), 207–238.

Moilanen, Inka, 'The Concept of the Three Orders of Society and Mobility in Eleventh-Century England', *English Historical Review*, 131 (2016), 1331–1352.

Molyneaux, George, 'The *Ordinance concerning the Dunsæte* and the Anglo-Welsh Frontier in the Late Tenth and Eleventh Centuries', *Anglo-Saxon England*, 40 (2011), 249–272.

Naismith, Rory, 'Gilds, States and Societies in the Early Middle Ages', *Early Medieval Europe*, 28 (2020), 627–662.

   'The Moneyers and Domesday Book', *Anglo-Norman Studies*, 45 (2022), 181–274.

   'The Ely Memoranda and the Economy of the Late Anglo-Saxon Fenland', *Anglo-Saxon England*, 45 (2017), 333–377.

   'The Land Market and Anglo-Saxon Society', *Historical Research*, 89 (2016), 9–41.

Niles, John D., 'Exeter Book Riddle 74 and the Play of the Text', *Anglo-Saxon England*, 27 (1998), 169–207.

O'Brien, Bruce, 'Authority and Community', in Julia Crick and Elisabeth Van Houts (eds.), *A Social History of England* (Cambridge: Cambridge University Press, 2011), 76–97.

Oexle, Otto Gerhard, 'Le travail au XIe siècle: Réalités et mentalités', in Jacquline Hamesse and Colette Muraille-Samaran (eds.), *Le travail au moyen âge: Une approche interdisciplinaire. Actes du colloque international de Louvain-la-Neuve, 21–23 mai 1987* (Louvain: Publications de l'Institut d'Études Médiévales, 1990), 49–60.

Oliver, Lisi, 'Wergild, Mund and Manbot in Early Anglo-Saxon Law', in Lukas Bothe, Stefan Esders, and Han Nijdam (eds.), *Wergild, Compensation and Penance: The Monetary Logic of Early Medieval Conflict Resolution* (Leiden: Brill, 2021), 113–132.

Osherson, Daniel N., and Edward E. Smith, 'On the Adequacy of Prototype Theory as a Theory of Concepts', *Cognition*, 9 (1981), 35–58.

Oxford English Dictionary Online. Oxford University Press. www.oed.com.

Padel, Oliver, *Slavery in Saxon Cornwall: The Bodmin Manumissions* (Cambridge: Anglo-Saxon, Norse and Celtic, 2009).

Pelteret, David, *Slavery in Early Medieval England* (Woodbridge: Boydell & Brewer, 1995).

Powell, Timothy E., 'The "Three Orders" of Society in Anglo-Saxon England', *Anglo-Saxon England*, 23 (1994), 103–132.

Pracy, Stuart, '"Medeman Mannum": Middling Sorts and Social Mobility in Early Medieval England, 900–1100', unpublished PhD thesis, University of Manchester (2020).

'Social Mobility and Manumissions in Early Medieval England', *Haskins Society Journal*, 31 (2020), 1–19.

Pratt, David, 'Demesne Exemption from Royal Taxation in Anglo-Saxon and Anglo-Norman England', *English Historical Review*, 128 (2013), 1–34.

Probert, Duncan, 'Exeter's Gildship and Manumission Records', in Steven Bassett and Alison J. Spedding (eds.), *Names, Texts and Landscapes in the Middle Ages: A Memorial Volume for Duncan Probert* (Donnington: Shaun Tyas, 2022), 21–38.

'Peasant Personal Names and Bynames from Late-Eleventh-Century Bury St Edmunds', *Nomina*, 37 (2014), 35–71.

Rabin, Andrew, *Crime and Punishment in Anglo-Saxon England* (Cambridge: Cambridge University Press, 2020).

'Old English *Forespeca* and the Role of the Advocate in Old English Law', *Mediaeval Studies*, 69 (2007), 223–254.

Old English Legal Writings (Cambridge, MA: Harvard University Press, 2020).

The Political Writings of Archbishop Wulfstan of York (Manchester: Manchester University Press, 2015).

Reuter, Timothy, 'The Medieval Nobility in Twentieth Century Historiography' in M. Bentley (ed.), *Companion to Historiography* (London: Routledge, 1997), 177–202.

Rigby, Stephen, *English Society in the Later Middle Ages: Class, Status and Gender* (London: Palgrave, 1995).

'Historical Materialism, Social Structure, and Social Change in the Middle Ages', *Journal of Medieval and early Modern Studies*, 34 (2004), 473–522.

Rio, Alice, '"Half-Free" Categories in the Early Middle Ages: Fine Status Distinctions before Professional Lawyers', in Judith Scheele and Paul Dresch (eds.), *Legalism: Rules and Categories* (Oxford: Oxford University Press, 2015), 129–152.

Slavery after Rome, 500–1100 (Oxford: Oxford University Press, 2017).

Roach, Levi, *Kingship and Consent in Anglo-Saxon England, 871–978: Assemblies and the State in the Early Middle Ages* (Cambridge: Cambridge University Press, 2013).

'Law Codes and Legal Norms in Later Anglo-Saxon England', *Historical Research*, 86 (2013), 465–486.

Robertson, Agnes J., *Anglo-Saxon Charters* (Cambridge: Cambridge University Press, 1956).

Rosch, Eleanor, 'Cognitive Representations of Semantic Categories', *Journal of Experimental Psychology: General*, 104 (1975), 192–233.

Rose-Troup, Frances, 'Exeter Manumissions and Quittances of the Eleventh and Twelfth Centuries', *Reports and Transactions of the Devonshire Association*, 69 (1937), 417–445.

Rosser, Gervasse, 'The Anglo-Saxon Gilds', in John Blair (ed.), *Minsters and Parish Churches: The Local Church in Transition 950–1200* (Oxford: Oxford University Committee for Archaeology, 1988), 31–34.

Rubin, Miri, 'Small Groups: Identity and Solidarity in the Late Middle Ages', in Jennifer Kermode (ed.), *Enterprise and Individuals in Fifteenth Century England* (Stroud: Alan Sutton, 1991), 132–150.

Schofield, Phillipp R., *Peasant and Community in Medieval England, 1200–1500* (London: Palgrave Macmillan, 2002).

Senecal, Christine, 'Keeping Up with the Godwinesons: In Pursuit of Aristocratic Status in Late Anglo-Saxon England', *Anglo-Norman Studies*, 23 (2001), 251–265.

Smith, Scott Thompson, *Land and Book: Literature and Land Tenure in Anglo-Saxon England* (Toronto: University of Toronto Press, 2012).

Stafford, Pauline, *Unification and Conquest: A Political and Social History of England in the Tenth and Eleventh Centuries* (New York: E. Arnold, 1989).

Stattel, Jake, 'Legal Culture in the Danelaw: A Study of III Æthelred', *Anglo-Saxon England*, 48 (2019), 163–203.

Stenton, Frank, 'The Thriving of the Anglo-Saxon Ceorl', in Doris Maris Senton (ed.), *Preparatory to Anglo-Saxon England* (Oxford: Oxford University Press, 1970), 383–393.

The First Century of Anglo-Saxon Feudalism: 1066–1166 (Oxford: Oxford University Press, 1979).

Stocker, David, 'Aristocrats, Burghers and Their Markets: Patterns in the Foundation of Lincoln's Urban Churches', in D. M. Hadley and Letty ten Harkel (eds.), *Everyday Life in Viking-Age Towns: Social Approaches to Towns in England and Ireland, c.800–1100* (Oxford: Oxbow Books, 2013), 119–143.

'Monuments and Merchants: Irregularities in the Distribution of Stone Sculpture in Lincolnshire and Yorkshire in the Tenth Century', in Dawn Hadley and Julian D. Richards (eds.), *Cultures in Contact: Scandinavian Settlement in England in the Ninth and Tenth Centuries* (Turnhout: Brepols, 2000), 179–212.

Stone, Rachel, *Morality and Masculinity in the Carolingian Empire* (Cambridge: Cambridge University Press, 2011).

Sukhino-Khomenko, Denis, '"Thrymsa, a Coin [Not] in Circulation in Northern England": Source Criticism of Archbishop Wulfstan's *Norðleoda laga* and Its Monetary Systems in the Way of Social History (England, 10–11th Centuries)', *Proslogion: Studies in Medieval and Early Modern Social History and Culture*, 6 (2021), 8–41.

Sykes, Naomi, 'Deer, Land, Knives and Halls: Social Change in Early Medieval England', *Antiquaries Journal*, 90 (2010), 175–193.

Talbot, C. H., ed. and trans., *The Life of Christina of Markyate: A Twelfth Century Recluse* (Oxford: Oxford University Press, 1987).

Taylor, John, *Linguistic Categorization: Prototypes in Linguistic Theory*, 2nd edition (Oxford: Clarendon, 1989).

Thorn, Frank, 'Non Pascua sed Pastura: The Changing Choice of Terms in Domesday', in David Roffe and S. B. Keats-Rohan (eds.), *Domesday Now: New Approaches to the Inquest and Book* (Woodbridge: Boydell & Brewer, 2016), 109–136.

Thorpe, Benjamin, ed. and trans., *Diplomatarium Anglicum Ævi Saxonici* (London: Macmillan, 1865).

Treharne, Elaine, 'The Conners of Exeter, 1070–1150', in E. J. Christie (ed.), *The Wisdom of Exeter: Anglo-Saxon Studies in Honour of Patrick W. Conner* (Berlin: De Gruyter, 2020), 11–26.

Upchurch, Robert K., 'A Big Dog Barks: Ælfric of Eynsham's Indictment of the English Pastorate and *Witan*', *Speculum*, 85 (2010), 505–533.

Webley, Robert, 'Conquests and Continuity: Portable Metalwork in Late Anglo-Saxon and Anglo-Norman England, *c*.AD 1000–1200', unpublished PhD thesis, University of York (2020).

Weikert, Katherine, 'Of Pots and Pins: The Households of Late Anglo-Saxon Faccombe Netherton', in Ben Jervis (ed.), *The Middle Ages Revisited: Studies in the Archaeology and History of Medieval Southern England Presented to Prof. David A. Hinton* (Oxford: Archaeopress, 2018), 58–70.

Whitelock, Dorothy, ed. and trans., *English Historical Documents I, c.500– 1042* (London: Eyre and Spottiswoode, 1968).

Williams, Ann, 'A Bell-House and a Burh-Geat: Lordly Residences in England before the Norman Conquest', in Robert Liddiard (ed.), *Anglo-Norman Castles* (Woodbridge: Boydell Press, 2003), 23–40.

'A Place in the Country: Orc of Abbotsbury and Tole of Tolpuddle, Dorset', in Ryan Lavelle and Simon Roffey (eds.), *The Danes in Wessex: The Scandinavian Impact on Southern England, c.800–c.1100* (Oxford: Oxbow Books, 2016), 158–171.

The World before Domesday: The English Aristocracy 900–1066 (London: Continuum, 2008).

Winterbottom, M., and R. Thomson, *Gesta pontificum Anglorum: The History of English Bishops*, vol. 2, iv.148.4–5 (Oxford: Oxford University Press, 2007).

Wormald, Patrick, 'Anglo-Saxon Law and Scots Law', *Scottish Historical Review*, 88 (2009), 192–206.

'Conclusion', in W. Davies and P. Fouracre (eds.), *The Settlement of Disputes in Medieval Europe* (Cambridge: Cambridge University Press, 1986), 207–240.

'Giving God and King Their Due: Conflict and Its Regulation in the Early English State', in *Legal Culture in the Early Medieval West: Law as Text, Image and Experience* (London: Hambledon, 1999), 333–357.

'Lordship and Justice in the Early English Kingdom: Oswaldslow Revisited', in *Legal Culture in the Early Medieval West: Law as Text, Image and Experience* (London: Hambledon, 1999), 313–332.

'*On þa wæpnedhealfe*: Kingship and Royal Property from Æthewulf to Edward the Elder', in Nicholas J. Higham and David H. Hill (eds.), *Edward the Elder, 899–924* (London: Routledge, 2001), 264–279.

Papers Preparatory to the Making of English Law: King Alfred to the Twelfth Century, vol. 2 (London: University of London, 2014).

Acknowledgements

I wish to express my gratitude to Megan Cavell, Rory Naismith, Winfried Rudolf, and Emily Thornbury for inviting me to contribute a volume on hierarchy to the Elements in England in the Early Medieval World series. I would especially like to express my appreciation to Rory for his guidance and patience throughout the editing process. Further thanks must go to Elizabeth Friend-Smith and the rest of those at Cambridge University Press who worked on this Element.

Special thanks are due as well to Emily Harless, Levi Roach, and Charles West for commenting on various (and, at times, quite different) iterations of this Element. Any mistakes that remain are, of course, entirely my own. This Element is dedicated to my father, Robert, who fostered my enduring interest in history.

Cambridge Elements ⁞

England in the Early Medieval World

Megan Cavell

University of Birmingham

Megan Cavell is Associate Professor in Medieval English Literature at the University of Birmingham. She works on a wide range of topics in medieval literary studies, from Old and early Middle English and Latin languages and literature to riddling, gender and animal studies. Her previous publications include *Weaving Words and Binding Bodies: The Poetics of Human Experience in Old English Literature* (2016), *Riddles at Work in the Early Medieval Tradition: Words, Ideas, Interactions* (co-edited with Jennifer Neville, 2020), and *The Medieval Bestiary in England: Texts and Translations of the Old and Middle English Physiologus* (2022).

Rory Naismith

University of Cambridge

Rory Naismith is Professor of Early Medieval English History in the Department of Anglo-Saxon, Norse and Celtic at the University of Cambridge, and a Fellow of Corpus Christi College, Cambridge. Also a Fellow of the Royal Historical Society, he is the author of *Early Medieval Britain 500–1000* (Cambridge University Press, 2021), *Citadel of the Saxons: The Rise of Early London* (2018), *Medieval European Coinage, with a Catalogue of the Coins in the Fitzwilliam Museum, Cambridge, 8: Britain and Ireland c. 400–1066* (Cambridge University Press, 2017) and *Money and Power in Anglo-Saxon England: The Southern English Kingdoms 757–865* (Cambridge University Press, 2012, which won the 2013 International Society of Anglo-Saxonists First Book Prize).

Winfried Rudolf

University of Göttingen

Winfried Rudolf is Chair of Medieval English Language and Literature in the University of Göttingen (Germany). Recent publications include *Childhood and Adolescence in Anglo-Saxon Literary Culture* (with Susan E. Irvine, 2018). He has published widely on homiletic literature in early England and is currently principal investigator of the ERC-Project ECHOE–Electronic Corpus of Anonymous Homilies in Old English.

Emily V. Thornbury

Yale University

Emily V. Thornbury is Associate Professor of English at Yale University. She studies the literature and art of early England, with a particular emphasis on English and Latin poetry. Her publications include *Becoming a Poet in Anglo-Saxon England* (Cambridge, 2014), and, co-edited with Rebecca Stephenson, *Latinity and Identity in Anglo-Saxon Literature* (2016). She is currently working on a monograph called *The Virtue of Ornament*, about pre-Conquest theories of aesthetic value.

About the Series

Elements in England in the Early Medieval World takes an innovative, interdisciplinary view of the culture, history, literature, archaeology and legacy of England between the fifth and eleventh centuries. Individual contributions question and situate key themes, and thereby bring new perspectives to the heritage of early medieval England. They draw on texts in Latin and Old English as well as material culture to paint a vivid picture of the period. Relevant not only to students and scholars working in medieval studies, these volumes explore the rich intellectual, methodological and comparative value that the dynamic researchers interested in England between the fifth and eleventh centuries have to offer in a modern, global context. The series is driven by a commitment to inclusive and critical scholarship, and to the view that early medieval studies have a part to play in many fields of academic research, as well as constituting a vibrant and self-contained area of research in its own right.

Cambridge Elements ☰

England in the Early Medieval World

Elements in the Series

A full series listing is available at: www.cambridge.org/EASW

Printed in the United States
by Baker & Taylor Publisher Services